everyday enlightenment

Why you don't have to become
a monk for meditation to
change your life

everyday enlightenment

everyday enlightenment
everyday enlightenment
everyday enlightenment
everyday enlightenment
everyday enlightenment
everyday enlightenment

LUKE McLEOD

NOTE TO READERS: This book contains advice arising from the personal experiences of the author and must not be treated as a substitute for the advice of qualified mental health practitioners. Neither the author nor the publisher can be held responsible for any loss or claim arising out of the use, or misuse, of the suggestions made or the failure to take professional advice.

hachette AUSTRALIA

Published in Australia and New Zealand in 2023
by Hachette Australia
(an imprint of Hachette Australia Pty Limited)
Gadigal Country, Level 17, 207 Kent Street, Sydney, NSW 2000
www.hachette.com.au

Hachette Australia acknowledges and pays our respects to the past, present and future Traditional Owners and Custodians of Country throughout Australia and recognises the continuation of cultural, spiritual and educational practices of Aboriginal and Torres Strait Islander peoples. Our head office is located on the lands of the Gadigal people of the Eora Nation.

A catalogue record for this book is available from the National Library of Australia

ISBN: 978 0 7336 5020 8 (paperback)

Cover design by Christabella Designs
Typeset in 12.5/18.5pt Cochin by Kirby Jones
Printed and bound in Australia by McPherson's Printing Group

The paper this book is printed on is certified against the Forest Stewardship Council® Standards. McPherson's Printing Group holds FSC® chain of custody certification SA-COC-005379. FSC® promotes environmentally responsible, socially beneficial and economically viable management of the world's forests.

This book is dedicated to you. May it bring you some relief, healing and happiness.

Contents

Introduction

'Have I been a good dad?'

It was mid-morning on just another Thursday. My two brothers, sister and I were sitting down with our dad in the cafeteria of a hospital in Sydney's Lower North Shore. He had just come out of triple by-pass heart surgery. The surgery went well but during the scans in preparation for his operation, the doctors had found some abnormal marks in his lungs. We didn't know yet whether or not this was cancer.

As I heard these words tremble past his lips, I'll never forget the look in his eyes. I sensed that his whole life was flashing through his mind, leaving him in a state of pure, vulnerable self-awareness.

At first I didn't know how to respond. I was conflicted inside. There was a part of me that obviously felt sad but there was another part that felt angry.

Why does it take the fear of death to finally value the gift of life?

I took a deep breath and knew I couldn't be honest with him at that time. 'Not now, Dad,' I said. 'Let's find out what's going on and we'll chat about this later.' It was also at that moment I made a promise to myself that I would do whatever I could to avoid ending up with the same look in my eyes which I saw so vividly in my father's eyes that day.

Maybe you've seen a similar look in a loved one's eyes, or possibly experienced moments yourself that have left you asking, 'Am I really happy?', 'What is the purpose of life?', 'What is this all for?' Maybe one of these questions is the reason why you picked up this book. Regardless of when they happen or whatever reason sparks these moments of self-reflection, I have no doubt that at some point, if not multiple points, in our life, every one of us will encounter them and will be given the opportunity to face some version of these life-altering questions.

I obviously don't know how old you are or what you've gone through in your life up until this point and in some ways this is a good thing, because it means we can start this journey together here and now, on a clean slate. All I can give you is some assurance that, from what I've experienced myself and seen in others, including my dad, taking the time to *literally* sit down and figure out the answers to these big questions, and then acting on them when they arise, is what determines whether or not we end up living a fulfilling, happy life. The hard part is, most of us are infected with a debilitating disease which stops us from doing this …

UNAWAREITIS

Most of us have become very unwell and we don't even know it. I call this disease *'unawareitis'*. It's a deep lack of awareness that has taken over our sense of self and slowly, over the course of our lives, deteriorates our mind, body and soul, and heavily impacts our quality of life. It's something that is very hard to detect and usually results in one of two serious side-effects:

- Insatiability: being incapable of being satisfied. Symptoms include – constant underlying feeling of anxiety, blind obsessions with the pursuit of either money, fame and/or power, fear of missing out (FOMO).
- Incognisance: being oblivious to one's internal environment (feelings, emotions and responses) and external environment (other people's feelings, behaviours and generally the world

around us). Symptoms include feeling lost and complacent, lack of accountability, often turning to stimulants (alcohol, social media, etc) to feel or suppress something.

Let's take a closer look at each of these, because if you're really wanting to get something out of this book, it's going to have to start with being really honest with yourself.

Insatiability

'Brother, you up yet? I need to talk to you.'

I had worked with Trev on and off in different businesses for the past ten years or so. He was, and still is, a very driven and determined person. A hunter is what I believe you'd call him in the business world. He is very successful from the outside perspective. Someone who has spent most of his life working extremely hard to attain a level of status and wealth that, to be honest, most of us would dream of. But on receiving this sms at 5.30 am on a Sunday, it was obvious that something was wrong.

Twenty minutes later I was standing out the front of my place as Trev drove up.

'You okay, mate?' I asked, looking at him and knowing by the heavy bags under his eyes that he wasn't.

'No, I don't think so, mate. Jane wants a divorce.'

Trev seemed to have it all, and yet there he was on

a Sunday morning standing in my driveway on the brink of a breakdown.

You've probably heard of a hundred similar stories to this. Maybe you've even experienced something similar yourself. I'll be the first here to put my hand up and say I've drunk the Kool Aid of insatiability. I've thought that the attainment of material wealth would bring me happiness. It doesn't and I think, deep down, we all know that. So the big question is, if we know this won't fulfil us, why then do we continue to pursue it? Because of unawareitis.

Over time we have become programmed not to suspect and doubt this way of living. Society has taught us that this should be the way we go about our lives. We try to keep up with our friends, neighbours or colleagues. Our whole environment has become obsessed with this pursuit. To the point where we have now accepted, either intentionally or reluctantly, that this is just the way it is and will continue to be. We have been fed this lie that happiness and fulfilment come through the attainment of things we don't have yet.

Now, let me be clear here: I'm not one of those folks who say you have to completely forgo all your ambition, move to the mountains and live off your homegrown veggies for the rest of your life (although that actually doesn't sound too bad). I understand the world we now live in. How we need a certain amount of money to provide for and take care of ourselves, family and loved ones. It would be foolish of me to think otherwise. What I do know for sure, though, is that once we start earning a certain amount of money, it can start to have a negative influence on our overall level of happiness. This is known as the 'Income Happiness Curve', and multiple studies have shown that there is a tipping point when it comes to wealth and its correlation with our wellbeing. In short, after we finally have enough, we begin to fear losing it. Which triggers us to want more. And more. And more. We become obsessed with the pursuit and the attachment to things. We let our ego take the steering wheel of our life and once it's left to its own free will, it can lead us down a path of false hope.

But again, don't get me wrong here. I don't believe our ego is the enemy and something to be suppressed or battled with, unlike what some others in the wellness space would have you believe. The way I see it, we were created with an ego, therefore it must serve a useful and beneficial purpose. Everything created from the natural world serves a purpose. If we treat our ego as our enemy and try to defeat it in some way, it will only come back with even more vengeance to serve out its purpose. Instead, we can learn to see it for what it is. We can understand its nature and purpose. How it is actually here to provide us with the necessary energy and ambition that is required for us to evolve and get closer to our true selves. But I'm getting ahead of myself here.

Let's come back to identifying some of the signs of insatiability. But before we do, just a little heads-up here. Some of these questions probably aren't going to make you feel all that good. They may even feel like you're being attacked a little. Acknowledging our own shortcomings is not an easy thing to do, but I assure you, being honest with ourselves here and whether we might be showing some of these signs is an essential and important step on this journey.

- Do you frequently compare yourself to others?
- Do you often feel like you are not good enough?
- Do you like gossip?
- Do you secretly enjoy it when others fail?
- Do you use sarcasm to make yourself feel better?
- Do you try to justify any of the above as 'just a joke'?

I warned you these questions weren't going to make you feel overly nice. An important point to make here is that if you were honest with yourself and answered yes to any of them, it's not your fault. We have been conditioned to think and act in these ways so that we can try to cope with the imbalance that insatiability has caused within us. It is, however, now your responsibility to do something about it.

Incognisance

Incognisance is when we are oblivious to how our thoughts, words and actions are affecting not only ourselves but all those around us too. It is a very sneaky condition that progresses quietly and covertly within. Starting off with subtle indicators, it eventually results in quite assertive and aggressive signs.

Let's go to the more intensive end of the spectrum first. One of the clear signs that someone has reached this point is a complete lack of accountability. Nothing seems to be their fault. They genuinely struggle to see things from another person's perspective and if they are confronted about this, they will become quite self-defensive and/or shut down. This results in them indulging in some type of self-pity or sabotage act. It is near impossible for someone at this stage to become aware of their own situation as the very nature of what has caused it is incognisance itself.

Identifying early signs is therefore essential. However, these aren't that easy to see either. I call them the 'quiet killers'. It starts with an inner whisper that something isn't quite right, warning you that something is a bit off. These could be thoughts like 'Hey, you don't deserve to be treated like that and deserve better', or 'You need to speak up more if this type of work is going to fulfil you.' If the time isn't taken to listen and act on these whispers, they will manifest into feelings of uncertainty and anxiety. These will continue to intensify until the mind either experiences a *breakthrough*, where you finally allow yourself to be present, listen and take action on what that inner voice is asking of you, or a *breakdown*, where the mind finally submits and accepts this state of inner unrest as normality.

You can see people in this unfortunate state everywhere. They are in this almost zombie-like mode, where it looks like the life has drained from their eyes. You can see that they've now just accepted this type of lifeless state as their fate. It's heartbreaking. I have found myself falling into this state multiple times throughout my life. The hardest and most important part is being able to realise and admit you've found yourself in this state. The good news (and it doesn't matter how old you are) is that you have the ability to notice this and turn things around. You don't have to accept this lifeless state. The cure is found within the steps of this book but first, let's look at how we got into all this mess to start with.

The Triple S Threat

Although there are thousands of contributing factors to unawareitis, I've tried to roll most of them up into three main categories that I think are currently having the biggest influence on our mental functioning and wellbeing. Together, they are called the 'Triple S Threat'.

Social media

Let's start with the most topical and controversial one. Sure, social media has brought about an ability to connect with and reach more people. I have used and will continue to use social media for this reason. However, there is no doubt that it has also had one of the biggest impacts on the cognitive functioning and emotional wellbeing of humans within the last 50 years. In fact, some would say that it's had *the* biggest impact on us. Here in Australia we currently spend an average of 36 days a year just on social media. We pick up our phone around 215 times a day and scroll about 90 metres a day on it. This is equivalent to your thumbs climbing Mount Everest every 100 days or so.

It is little wonder then that we have now overtaken the notoriously ill-focused goldfish when it comes to our attention span. The pond-dwellers have an average attention span of around nine seconds. We're currently sitting at an impressive average of eight seconds. For all the wonderful things technology has done for us, this has to be one of its greatest tragedies. Intentional or not, the algorithms primarily created by social media companies have changed the way we think and operate.

There have now been conclusive studies done on how social media affects the brain, particularly around constantly triggering small releases of dopamine. The problem with this is that dopamine is like sugar for the brain. In small doses it's fine, even healthy. However, it is also extremely addictive and, therefore, if we have an unlimited, free source that provides access to it (have you ever reached the end of your TikTok or Instagram feed?), the mind will consume itself with it. The more time we spend in this virtual reality, the more detached we become from our *actual* reality. Regardless of how much these social media juggernauts will try to make us believe, we can't solely survive in the virtual space. We need contact and connection with the real world for our body, mind and soul to survive.

Social media has shattered our ability to focus. This is a skill, which we'll soon discover, that is essential for us to be able to provide ourselves with some much-needed peace of mind and relief.

Society/the system

Even when we do escape from the grasp of our phones, we are still surrounded with forces trying to push us into any place but here. Our society has been built to have us believe that we cannot be fulfilled without certain things: money, status, a big house, a loving partner, even spirituality and God. Yes, even the things that we think are good for us. All are based on the 'if you get that, then you will finally get this' assumption. This creates a constant underlying state of anxiety and fear. You are either anxious because you don't have what you think you should have or you're fearful of losing what you do have. We're either scrambling to hold on to something or clinging on to it once we've got it. This becomes incredibly exhausting as most of us haven't been shown another way so we just assume this is what life is meant to be like. Climb and cling. Climb and cling.

We may think then that the answer to not being caught up in this relentless cycle is to simply 'step off' the ride. Let go of the pursuit and of that which we are so attached to. But let's be really honest here. We can't do that. We don't live in a world that supports that action. I can't expect you to just walk away from your family, give up your job and everything you've worked so hard for. Nor do I want you to let go of your dreams and ambition of creating a life you want. Renunciation of what we want or have isn't the answer. Bringing awareness to the *attachment* we have with these belief systems is. Once we learn how to step back and see ourselves in the whole frame, to shine a light on the constant climb-and-cling story we're caught up in, we can then intentionally choose to change how we navigate through this journey. Rather than continuously climbing, we can now choose to explore wondrously without the fear of falling. Instead of desperately clinging on to that which we have worked for, we can choose to loosen our grip a little. Give yourself some space to be free and breathe.

One of the first pieces of advice most golf coaches will give you to improve your golf swing is, 'loosen your grip a little'. The same goes for life. Developing this greater level of awareness shows us whether we're playing the game of life or if life is actually playing us.

Suppressants

This is another tough one to admit and talk about but, as I said, these are what I believe to be the top three most pressing threats to us finding genuine happiness and fulfilment. So again, we have to be honest with ourselves by identifying what is holding us back and suppressants, particularly alcohol, is definitely one of them. 'Come on, Luke!' I hear you saying. 'First social media and now you're going to take my glass of wine away from me?'

Not entirely. I'm just here to point out what I deem to be the main causes and factors that are continuing to hold us down to be less than what we truly are and deserve.

You'll notice a common thread throughout this book where, rather than telling you what to do or not, I'm trying to, hopefully, bring some awareness of the influence and impact that these things are having on us. From here, you can make up your own mind about what you want to do. Even on this very topic I'd be a hypocrite if I was to tell you not to drink alcohol when I myself still enjoy a glass of wine now and then.

Isn't it interesting how even though we know something is bad for us, we'll still continue to do it. Why, though?

Well, in the case of alcohol, it can initially act as a form of relief and relaxation, which can feel nice at first. It has also become a way of bringing people together, a way to connect and socialise with our friends and family. These two initial positive aspects of alcohol can be quite alluring and addictive.

As I'm sure you're aware, though, the downside of these types of suppressants does definitely outweigh the positives – sorry. If you can completely renounce these suppressants, then all power to you. Would we all be better off without them? Yes. Is it my responsibility to tell you what you can and can't do? No. I just want to bring some awareness about this threat and highlight the impact it has on us and our ability to live an aware and fulfilling life.

Again, I don't want to get ahead of myself here but we will be delving into how we can begin to observe our relationship with things like alcohol, and anything for that matter, that is holding us back from being our true selves. In the meantime, here are a few questions to ponder on about this topic:

- Could you go a month or two without alcohol?
- How would your friends and family react if you were to take a break from it?

* Is the consumption of it affecting your relationships?
* Do you find you become a different person when you drink?
* Is it helping you be the best version of yourself?

All I'm asking for at this point is to be honest with yourself. There's no right or wrong answer, just an honest answer. Because if we're to go on this journey together, it's going to require a lot of not-so-comfortable moments of self-reflection.

But why bother?

We all end up in the same place, right? Six feet underground as worm food. Does it really matter how aware we become? Is it really worth finding and admitting all these things we need to work on within ourselves? Maybe it might be easier and less confronting if we just keep things how they are. Does all this really matter if we all end up having the same fate?

These are fair and reasonable points. I have asked myself these questions too. The short and direct answer is that it doesn't matter. Unless you want it to.

It's for you to figure out. Again, all I am suggesting is that you're honest with yourself. What do you feel when you ask yourself these questions?

The fact that you've picked up this book tells me that it does matter to you. That there's that whisper inside that just won't go away. A constant feeling of uncertainty and uneasiness. An undercurrent of anxiety. Something you just can't put your finger on and figure out. Why else would you be here with me at this moment? So it's completely up to you.

If it doesn't matter, feel free to put the book down and I wish you all the best with life.

If it does matter, great. Let's talk about that then.

The point of it all

Let's cut straight to the core. The point of every one of our lives is to experience it as much as possible. Yep, that's it. To live and experience life to the fullest. Now I know you might be thinking, 'You mean to tell me the whole cliché *of living life to the fullest* is all you've got?' Well, kind of.

First, most clichés become clichés for a reason. Second, what does it truly mean to *live* life to its fullest? Some might think it means doing whatever you want, whenever you want. Sounds pretty good, right? But even if you did have all the time and money in the world to do whatever you wanted, whenever you wanted, you're still going to fall short of living life to its fullest. We've all known or heard of people who seemingly had it all and could do whatever they wanted, and still somehow ended up either deeply depressed or completely lost. Is that living life to its fullest? Hardly.

Others might think that living life to its fullest means

achieving all their dreams and aspirations. Sorry to say, but this too will only get you so far. Again, the evidence of this shortfall is all around us. How many times have you seen someone who has worked really hard – or even done so yourself – to achieve something significant in their life, to then within a day or so after this achievement slip straight back into feelings of worry, doubt and anxiety?

To truly live a life to its fullest requires us to learn a whole new way of living altogether, as it becomes clear that what we've been trying isn't working. There are people who are already experiencing this genuine fullness in life. Sages, yogis and Zen masters have been doing so for centuries, but their way of living is unreasonable for most of us. Even a lot of their teachings are out of date and out of touch for where most of us are at in our lives. Can we take their wisdom, unpack it and make it work for us everyday folk though? Those of us who are working a 9-to-5 job with a mortgage and two kids, can we do that? I believe so. All the resources and tools they had to figure out this way of living, we have too. All we need now is someone to just make sense of it all and explain it in a way we can understand …

Well it's nice to meet you too :)

Enlightenup

These days, enlightenment is either seen as a grandiose, unattainable state that people seem scared to talk about or some mythical fairy dust reserved only for woke social media influencers. I was even nervous about having the word in the title of this book, as I thought it might deter some people from wanting to read it because of how the word is perceived by so many. Either way, we all need to lighten up about this whole enlightenment thing.

It's not some impossible state of being or a fluffy wellness trend. It's about working on yourself. Pulling back all the layers that have built up over time and getting yourself to a point that you feel calm, confident and content about yourself. It's about shining a light on yourself!

If we are to actually look at the breakdown of the word itself, it comes from the Latin prefix of *en*, meaning 'in or into', and *lux*, meaning light. Put these together and you have 'into the light'. Or I like to define it as 'shining a light on ourselves'. In other words, enlightenment is about seeing ourselves as we truly are, warts and all, and then doing something about it.

So now that we've shone a light on that, let's keep on moving.

What would
you prefer?
Have a breakdown
or meditate?

Most of our waking lives we are not 'here', we are usually 'in there'. In our heads. Thinking. Ruminating. Doubting. Questioning. Pretty much doing everything else but experiencing and living life. Completely unaware. Life is either passing us by as we carry on in our comfortable complacency or we're too busy grasping for the next 'thing' that we think will make us happy. I have only been able to find two ways out of this.

One is that something drastic has to happen to you. Something that really shakes you up and out of this oblivious state of being. As in, one of those moments that feels like a crack of thunder has suddenly struck you on top of your head. This could be the death of someone close to you, a serious health scare you encounter, a fire burning down your home. Yes, most of the time it needs to be this serious for us to really put things in perspective and change our way of being.

I'm begging you! Please don't wait for something that breaks you down in order for you to break through.

This is option one: a breakdown. An incident that has caused all your walls to fall in and forces you to dig your way out.

Of course, I wouldn't want this to happen to anyone but, unfortunately, it's either something like this has to happen or you can go the second way – you can start meditating. The choice of what we'd prefer between these two options almost seems absurd, right? However, most of us do go with option number one. Why? Because we're too unaware, comfortable and/or privileged to consider option number two. It's the truth. How many times have you said, or heard someone say, 'If only I ...'

I'm begging you! Please don't wait for something that breaks you down in order for you to break through. There is another way, and yes it is through meditation. I know you're probably saying, 'Really, Luke? Meditation is going to do that for me?' Yes it can and it will, if you let it. It mightn't be as sudden as a breakdown but, bit by bit, meditation will lift you out of this fog and expose the truth about everything around you and yourself. This is why it is often referred to as the vehicle to enlightenment. It will show you what really is important and how to live your life.

Similar to the term enlightenment, meditation is flogged everywhere these days. Unfortunately because of this, I feel its purpose and the power of what it can do has been dramatically diluted. Sure, the hype around it has brought more attention to it but like with most things that become the flavour of the month, it can tend to lose its potency. But with the proper guidance, approach and commitment, it can and will change your life.

How does it do this, though?

Put simply, it does this by unlocking our awareness. There is not a single more valuable thing you can do in your life than develop your own level of awareness. Awareness puts everything in perspective. It makes real and important priorities crystal clear. It shines a light on our insecurities. It provides us courage by being able to see the whole picture. It puts us in a state of being able to squeeze every last drop out of the precious life we've been given. So if you are willing and wanting to see what life can really be like, then strap yourself in because this will be quite the ride.

Welcome to your own Awareness Adventure!

In order for you to complete this obstacle course, you'll need to follow The Soul Alive Method. This method has been designed to awaken your true, hidden self that has been buried under all the conditioned layers you have been exposed to throughout your life. It directly targets the cause of unawareitis by putting yourself through three main stages: The Relief Stage, The Healing Stage and The Happiness Stage. Each stage will require commitment, patience and a healthy dose of curiosity. Shall we begin?

THE SOUL ALIVE METHOD

Stage One

RELIEF

Settle the mind and you will hear the soul speak.

When you find yourself in a hospital seriously ill or injured, what's one of the first things a doctor or nurse gives you? They give you something to ease the pain. A painkiller maybe, or a bandage to stop the bleeding. Whatever it takes just to give you some instant relief and keep you alive if the situation is bad enough. They certainly aren't talking to you during this time about what you should be eating to improve your health or recommending you see a psychologist to deal with the trauma that may have led you to this point. No. At this time it's 'Give me whatever I need to experience some relief!'

Whether we're willing to admit it or not, this is where most of us are in our everyday lives. We're unwell and are in need of some desperate relief. Therefore, it's pointless for me to talk about prevention tactics when we haven't even stopped the bleeding yet.

Meditation used as ‘first aid’

Meditation, first and foremost, is wonderful for pain relief for our inner wounds. It can be used to ease all the emotional cuts, bumps and bruises which our chaotic lives can cause, giving us some much-needed reprieve. When used only for this purpose, however, it's important to know that at this stage meditation is not going to fix the problems that cause these injuries to our wellbeing. Relief from them? Yes. Fix them? Not yet.

Using meditation initially to just experience some much-needed relief is almost essential. As you'll come to realise, it is near impossible to enter into stages two and three without first being able 'calm the farm' in your head. It will give you that instant relief that you've probably been looking for and if you keep at it, it will help you develop a stable, calm state of mind to then be able to observe, process and rewire your deeper emotional conditioning (which is what Stage Two and Stage Three are all about).

Relief meditation, which is what we're looking at here in Stage One, is also the safest and easiest form of meditation to undertake. So don't worry, it won't have you bawling your eyes out or in some deep trance state ... yet.

How does relief meditation work?

You may have heard how meditation quietens the mind. But meditation doesn't exactly quiet the mind, it shifts the mind. It puts the mind into a different gear and it just so happens that this gear is quite quiet.

I like to see our mind as a type of gearbox. Most of the time we're in drive mode, moving up and down through the gears, and what we're doing at the time will determine what gear we need to be in. Sometimes we're flying down the freeway in sixth and other times we find ourselves on a windy road which requires us to be constantly moving between second, third and fourth. We might also find ourselves in reverse, looking in the rear-vision mirror, trying to make sense of what's behind us.

This constant changing of gears, up and down, back and forth, inevitably takes its toll on our engine. Wearing it down. We're constantly told to be in gear. Pushing forward. Doing. Achieving. Faster! Faster! But there is one gear that provides some rare solace. One that hardly gets used. The neutral gear. This is the gear that relief meditation puts you into.

When you're in neutral, everything is still on and usable. However, the engine and the gearbox isn't getting flogged and you as the driver get a chance to look around and appreciate everything. Maybe the sun is setting over a mountain in the distance or you notice a breeze moving through the trees. It's giving you some time and space to breathe instead of having to concentrate only on the black bitumen with white lines in front of or behind you.

We move our mind into this neutral gear by connecting it with something in the present moment. That's it. This may sound simple but it is actually quite difficult to do for most of us, even just for a few seconds. Why? Because no one has shown us how to do it. In fact, we are raised and encouraged to spend most of our waking lives in either drive or reverse.

When we experience these 'moments of connection', whether intentionally or by accident, the mind slips into this space of ease and freedom. It becomes free from its job for a moment. The job of having to constantly think. Every part of us needs a break. Time to restore some balance. It's

When we experience these 'moments of connection', whether intentionally or by accident, the mind slips into this space of ease and freedom.

a law of nature and the mind is no exception. Engaging in some type of relief meditation intentionally puts the mind into neutral gear and literally gives you that much-needed break.

Remember, it's just a break. You're not going to solve anything here yet. That toxic relationship is still going to be there, or that stressful job, those bills that need to be paid, that weight that needs to be lost. I'm sorry, but all the challenges you have will still be there. This stage and type of meditation is purely designed to just give you a break from it all.

But a break can do a lot. It can give you the renewed energy you need to finally have that difficult conversation. The ability to focus on and complete that task at work that has been stressing you out for some time. The motivation to put on your sneakers and go for a walk. So even though 'it's just a break', never underestimate the power of what five to ten minutes spent in this neutral gear of the mind can do.

SHIFTING THE MIND INTO THE NEUTRAL GEAR THROUGH CONNECTION WITH BODILY SENSATIONS

Can you feel your toes?

As you are reading these words, your mind is in gear. It is engaging in work, consuming the words, interpreting and making sense of them. You might be kicking back on a comfy couch and feel quite relaxed but your mind is still in drive mode. What I'd like you to do is take a moment to see if you can *feel* your left big toe. I know that might sound a bit funny at first, but go with me here.

Allow your awareness to drift down into your left big toe. Take your time. You'll probably need to let your gaze soften a bit and move away from the book, which is totally fine.

Just focus on feeling your left big toe. What do you notice?

A tingling sensation? If so, does this sensation have a subtle throbbing rhythm to it or is it stable and constant? Does it spread or contract, or both? Do you feel heat or warmth there? Close your eyes for a moment and see if you notice any colour there?

Just observe. Be curious. Take in whatever you notice.

Okay. Congratulations! You just engaged in a relief meditation. You shifted your mind into the neutral gear just for a moment. Whatever you noticed doesn't matter. The fact that you noticed something is the key. If you didn't notice much, don't worry. Remember, this is something we're not used to doing and it's not a state we've learnt to be in. Take your time and have fun with this exercise. Bookmark this page and come back to it whenever you want to have a play with this type of meditation.

You can also do this meditation exercise with any part of your body. I find that my toes, the tips of my fingers and different parts of my face are the easiest to feel and notice. As you practise exploring these sensations, they will become more obvious and stronger, and then you can try directing whatever you notice to move throughout the rest of your body. For example, if you felt a type of tingling sensation in your left big toe when focusing on it, try to move that sensation to spread out across the rest of your toes on your left foot. Then move it over to your right foot. If the sensation changes, no worries, just take in whatever the new sensation feels like. Now invite it to move along the soles of your feet, then around your heels and up your legs. You can take it wherever you want to. Just keep feeling and noticing. That's all you need to do.

The more practice and fun you have with this meditation, the more you are developing your awareness ability and reserves. This is the first ingredient to curing unawareitis.

Primary and secondary connection senses

This body scan exercise isn't the only type of meditation that allows the mind to move into the neutral gear. You can engage your other senses to achieve the same outcome. Some of us may be more attuned to connecting with an auditory sensation. Others could be more visual. Start with trying to notice a physical sensation within the body (just like what we did with our big toes), then move your awareness to another sense – a sound you can hear, for example, and see which you can notice more easily and strongly.

I refer to this as finding your primary and secondary connection senses – when you have identified which of your senses you can use to most confidently and easily connect to the present moment. For example, I know for me that my primary connection sense is kinaesthetic, which means connecting with some type of physical sensation within the body. Another very common type of kinaesthetic meditation is feeling your breath moving in and out of your body. For this, I like to zoom into the small area just underneath my nostrils to feel the sensation of the air moving in and out of my nose.

My secondary connection sense is auditory. It's not as strong as my primary connection, so I mostly use it to support my kinaesthetic sense. Sometimes, though, I will just practise a complete auditory relief meditation to keep things fresh and interesting. But I know it's definitely my secondary sense.

Our taste and smell senses tend to be tricky senses to use as primary modes for meditation. It is difficult to stay connected to the present moment with either of these, because taste and smell can both change in intensity, form and function very quickly. So I suggest using these two senses as supportive booster senses for your primary connection, as a way of going deeper and experiencing more with your meditations. For example, let's use another bodily kinaesthetic connection point as our primary sense. This time it's our tongue. Take a moment to see if you can feel your tongue this very moment. What do you notice about it? You might notice the feeling of it touching the back of your upper teeth. Now can you relax the tongue into the bottom palate of your jaw? So the tongue spreads out along the bottom of your mouth. Can you feel the root of your tongue down your throat and relax it there? Now see if you can taste anything. Maybe it's a subtle bitterness in

The more practice and fun you have with this meditation, the more you are developing your awareness ability and reserves. This is the first ingredient to curing unawareitis.

the mouth left over from your morning coffee or the lining of saliva around your mouth. Are there any tastes you can pick up on?

Okay. You can come back now. See how taste can be used as a booster of another sense? However, if you were to use taste as your primary connection point it would be very difficult to notice (unless you are eating or drinking something) and even more difficult to maintain a connection with it (as it is constantly changing and/or fading).

So you're now left with determining whether your visual, auditory or kinaesthetic sense is your primary sense and which of these is your secondary sense. We've done a few quick kinaesthetic tests, let's now look at auditory and visual to see how they resonate with you. Remember, we are looking for what we notice the most easily and what is also the most notable sensation.

Auditory relief meditation

This type of connection sense usually takes the form of a mantra-based meditation or frequency meditation. Frequency meditation is where you listen to and connect with a specific sound frequency. You may have heard of labels like white, green and brown noise. These can be artificially produced or through sound bowls, chimes and drums.

A mantra-based meditation can be a phrase, sound or combination of words and letters that you repeat and connect with to move the mind into the neutral gear.

There is a lot of history and opinions when it comes to mantra meditation. You may have heard of Transcendental Meditation (TM), which is a branded type of auditory meditation that has gained popularity throughout the West due to its marketing and celebrity endorsements. Its origins mainly come from the Vedic traditions, which refers to the teachings and experiences of various lineages of sages who lived on the Indian subcontinent in ancient times. During the Vedic era, there was no organised religion so no one's way of thinking was controlled or guided by a set system of beliefs. I'm no expert in the teachings of Vedic but it's truly a fascinating rabbit hole to disappear into when you have some time.

The key thing I want to point out with this type of meditation is that it uses some form of auditory cue as the sense connection with the present moment. The most common mantra used from Vedic teachings is 'Om', which intentionally has no meaning. If it did, you would still be engaging the thinking mode of your mind. You would interpret it and/or create a story of the word, just like you're doing right now reading the words on this page. Therefore, your mind is still in gear and not in neutral. It is the *sound* and the *frequency* of the word that you are connecting with. This means that you are not thinking the word, you're *feeling* it.

There are thousands of different mantras you can use and when a mantra is repeated over a sustained period of time, it will shift the mind into the neutral gear. Variation of the mantra can have a different effect on the body and mind, too. Similar to what position you meditate in. Whether you want to relax or feel energised, there are different mantras to suit different occasions and needs. Even though some teachers can be quite strict with indoctrinating their students with a specific mantra for a set period of time, I tend to lean more towards encouraging you to explore all different types of meditation at varying lengths to see what you encounter. After all, that is what real life is like, constantly moving and changing, and by having a wider collection of assets you can choose from to access the neutral gear, it can only lead to a greater and deeper level of awareness.

Visual relief meditation

Visual relief meditation is the other main type of meditation I want to touch on here.

Recently I was doing a meditation session with a client, taking him through my usual process of discovering what his primary connection sense was. For me, visual cues have never been strong but for this person they were very prominent. When I asked what he noticed when he focused on his toes, it wasn't a tingling sensation (kinaesthetic), it was a colour. He said he could see a reddish colour. This was the first thing he noticed. A clear indicator that his primary sense was visual. We continued up throughout his body and he kept referencing that he noticed different colours in different parts of his body. He was able to vividly connect with and describe where and what these colours were. I was quite fascinated and amazed, as it is difficult for me to notice and connect with a visual reference. I made sure that he wasn't just seeing these colours in his imagination but actually feeling and connecting with the colour in that specific part of his body. He assured me that he could definitely feel the colour and described the nature and detail of it.

To learn whether a visual connection sense is your primary sense, try doing the same body scan I took you through, but this time close your eyes and when focusing on your left big toe, see if you notice a colour there. If you do and it's quite obvious, great! Go explore it. Zoom into the colour. What else do you notice about it? Does the colour change at all? Does it move? Vibrate? Can you direct the colour to different parts of your body? What happens then?

What's important here is that you can actually see and feel the colour in that area of your body, not just *think* or *imagine* it. For some of you this may almost seem silly. It is actually difficult for me to notice these colours as I know it's not my primary connection sense. But I now know for sure that there are those of you who are completely on board with this and will notice certain colours as soon as you close your eyes.

* * *

Whatever sense you choose to explore and connect with, it doesn't matter. They all lead to and provide the same thing – a sanctuary for your mind. That neutral gear that will give you that needed relief and *peace of mind,* even if

There are thousands of different mantras you can use and when a mantra is repeated over a sustained period of time, it will shift the mind into the neutral gear.

you just start with a moment or two. So find out what your primary connection sense is and then use your other secondary connection senses to support and go deeper with your practice.

Let's not forget the other huge benefit we are establishing here. When we consistently practise these types of meditations, along with using them for relief when we need it, we are building our base level of awareness. We are rewiring our brains and laying a new mental foundation that will be our bedrock for building a new life full of awareness.

The usual hurdles

To be able to fully navigate your way through this new world of awareness and set you up as best as possible to enter into Stage Two (Healing) of the journey, there are going to be inevitable hurdles you will have to overcome. The following will help you tremendously in doing this.

Set aside the spiritual stuff and first get practical

One thing I've noticed in the wellbeing space is that people spend a lot of time talking about the experience and little about the practical process to achieving the experience. I know they are well intentioned when they talk about their 'enlightening' encounters and this can at times be very motivating and inspiring to hear, but I am often left asking myself, 'That sounds amazing and I'm happy for you, but how do I get there too?' And when you do ask for practical advice, the usual answer is something along the lines of, 'Just relax. Everything is going to be okay.' This response, although it does have a deep truth to it, usually achieves the exact opposite of its intention. Especially if it is said to someone who is at the beginning of their meditation journey.

It gives off this carefree attitude that you should develop an aversion to practicality and structure. There's this 'Just let it be, man' vibe. This type of 'vibe' and advice is rarely helpful to the everyday person who has hundreds of regular responsibilities and commitments to keep up.

Hand on heart, one of the two things that made the biggest difference to my journey of this whole 'developing awareness' ride was when I started adding meditation to my daily to-do list. (The other was when I shifted how I approached meditation. More on this is on page 91.) The day I started treating meditation as a daily priority, and not just something I did when I was stressed or anxious, was when I really noticed this 'peace of mind' attitude starting to develop. In fact, a lot of the time I would actually recommend NOT meditating when you're feeling this way, which we'll also cover in an upcoming chapter. However you organise and 'tick off' what you need to get done each day, add ten minutes of meditation to your to-do list, starting from tomorrow. I honestly couldn't be more serious about this. It will hands-down be one of the best decisions you'll make in your life.

The importance of this simple, practical step really hit home for me when I realised that each day we will naturally be exposed to stress. Whether that's having to deal with a difficult task or situation at work, looking after a screaming baby or putting together the latest IKEA flat-pack. Stress is inevitable. Relief, however, is not. The only time the mind and the body naturally relaxes and unwinds each day is when we go to sleep. Even then that can be difficult for a lot of us. So if we don't treat relief

However you organise and 'tick off' what you need to get done each day, add ten minutes of meditation to your to-do list, starting from tomorrow.

in a very practical manner, it won't actually happen. Yet I can guarantee you'll still be exposed to stress every day whether you want it or not and if we don't fight to restore this balance, that stress will continue to snowball until the mind and the body begin to break down or, as it's more commonly known, we end up 'burnt out'.

Skills before pills

Meditation is a skill and therefore something we can all learn. Just like learning to ride a bike, you can learn how to meditate. Yes, it does require some effort and patience but anyone can learn how to do it. But here lies a bit of a problem. Effort and patience are two qualities we are increasingly in short supply of. When everyone and everything around us is pushing for things to be done faster and more efficiently, we begin to take things for granted and expect that these new fast and efficient options are the best. Low in iron levels? Just pop an iron vitamin and you'll be right! Need something frozen quickly? No worries, chuck it in the blast chiller.

Now, there's nothing wrong with being able to make ice cream in under 15 minutes. The point is that we're constantly being told, and marketed to, that the easiest option is also the best option. But this isn't necessarily the case with everything. Especially when it comes to dealing with our emotions and state of mind. Yet we are still being told that there are 'easy options' for dealing with these challenges.

Let me be clear here. Medicine and medication are some of the most incredible inventions in human history.

They have saved billions of lives and will continue to do so. I also have the utmost respect and admiration for clinical doctors and practitioners for the work they do and for all the lives they have saved through their recommendations and prescriptions. I am, however, nervous about how quickly we, as a society, have accepted that swallowing a pill or two is going to fix everything. Again, don't get me wrong. For many people, medication IS the appropriate course of action. For many others, though, in my opinion, we should be considering and recommending more extensive and practical solutions first, like learning how to meditate. Especially when it comes to behavioural disorders.

Canadian physician Dr Gabor Maté shares some wonderful insights on how certain behavioural disorders, such as ADHD, are learnt over time from exposure to stress and develop as a mental safety mechanism to actually protect the mind. This therefore, in some ways, is a skill that is learnt. What a fascinating perspective. That something like ADHD is seen as a learnt skill to protect the self. It is then that this learnt skill begins to work against us. By increasing our dopamine levels, however, we are able to restore this balance. This is what ADHD medication does. It has also been proven, though, that meditation can also increase dopamine levels within the brain. For me, it makes a lot more sense to at least try to learn a skill like meditation to counteract this chemical imbalance first. This way we're not just treating ourselves, we're training ourselves to heal and restore the balance.

Make it a treat

Growing up in country New South Wales, my two brothers, my sister and I spent a lot of time outdoors testing out the durability of our bodies and wellbeing. Whether it was climbing trees, racing motorbikes or the odd brotherly 'friendly' scrap. Plus, my older brother was twice my size, so I got injured a lot. When I would make my way home holding another injury of some sort, crying out to Mum for help, she had this wonderful trick of giving me some pain relief, usually a Panadol. She would crush it up on a teaspoon and mix it with some honey so it would taste better and I could swallow it. It made the whole process of taking the medicine a lot easier and more enjoyable. Meditation is often just seen as a pill you should swallow now and then to ease the pain and, although I think there's nothing wrong with using meditation in this way, you're going to enjoy it more and therefore stick with it if you begin to see it as a treat for yourself rather than a means to an end.

This was the second thing that made the biggest impact on my meditation practice: when I started seeing it as something I wanted to do rather than should do. I now love meditating. It's something I look forward to. It's like I get to have my favourite meal every day. By seeing meditation in this light, you begin to notice similarities with the other things you love to do in your life and it will soon become another habit that brings you pleasure and happiness.

A great way to implement this type of approach and perspective to meditation is to start seeing it as an inner adventure. So each time you close your eyes to meditate, feel as if you're about to go and explore a new world. What am I going to stumble upon this time? Can I find something new to connect with the present moment that I've never noticed before? What emotion is going to arise that wants my attention? How am I going to respond to the inevitable chatter that will pop into my head at some point during this time? Taking this approach, it's like you've wandered into an enchanted forest, full of new, fascinating plants, animals and scenery, and there you are, just taking it all in, wide-eyed in awe and wonder. Then, meditation becomes this fascinating, wonderful adventure, not just some chore you have to do or a pill you have to take. It's a joy. This approach to meditation is something that has profoundly changed the way I see and experience meditation. It also makes it a whole lot more fun!

Set a goal for the number of times you would like to meditate each week and strive for that. The neutral gear of the mind is achieved by releasing effort, not applying it.

Falling into the moment

One of the most fascinating things about meditation is how it achieves its objective. This is unlike how we accomplish most things in life where we set a goal (lose 5 kilos, get a promotion, buy a house) and then apply effort to achieving it (exercise, work hard, save). The neutral gear of the mind is achieved via the exact reverse order to this. You start by *releasing* effort, not by applying it. By stepping down, not up. Then after a period of time of doing this *letting go*, you arrive at your destination. This is what trips up most people when starting out with meditation. They go about it just like they would when learning new skills or setting out to achieve the goals in their lives, and why wouldn't they? That's the formula we've followed to achieve pretty much everything else in our lives. However, using this approach to achieve the outcome of meditation will only lead to frustration and annoyance.

Use the traditional approach of achievement for everything else leading up to and after meditation. For example, feel free to set a goal for the number of times you would like to meditate each week and strive for that. But as soon as you sit down to meditate and your eyes close, it's time to let go and surrender to the moment.

Sleep is one of the very few other things that is achieved in a similar fashion. The harder we try to sleep, the less likely it's going to happen. Hence the reason we call it *falling* asleep. When we finally *drop* whatever we're thinking about, our lights go out (or maybe a more accurate way to put it is, our lights finally 'turn on').

Some of you will be asking, 'Isn't there effort required in directing and returning your focus during meditation?' There's a big difference between strenuous focus and curious observation. In meditation we are not trying to hold on to the present moment, we are simply observing, in awe of it. In other words, we are *falling* into the moment, and the more we continually 'let go', the more relief we will experience.

Sleep and meditation

Sleep and meditation are like identical twins working at the same restaurant. They look the same, speak the same and are providing the same type of service to you – to give you some relief, rest and time to recharge. So close are they that sometimes the body and the brain can't tell the difference. That's why a lot of people often feel sleepy or actually fall asleep during meditation. If you fall asleep during meditation, great. It's what you needed and certainly something you shouldn't beat yourself up over if you do nod off during your practice. Relief is relief and it doesn't matter to me how that is served up. If it's what I need and it's on offer, I'll take it, thanks.

If the reason that has led you to this book is that you're in search of relief, if you're feeling burnt out, stressed and/or anxious and need some relief from it, then there is nothing better that will provide this for you than sleep. If this is the case, use meditation first and foremost to complement and improve your sleep before trying to achieve anything else from it. Start by doing a ten-minute body scan meditation before bed each night to help you fall asleep. By improving your sleep as your first port of call, you will receive the necessary energy to operate effectively throughout your day. Once your energy levels are replenished enough through sleep, you can then use meditation as a vehicle to explore other realms of developing and improving yourself.

Meditation can do a lot but it can't do it all

Meditation is often only introduced to people when they have reached a breaking point. It could be your doctor recommending you should try it after finding that your blood pressure is too high, or maybe a friend has noticed how visibly stressed you seem. Although meditation can be and is a wonderful SOS relief exercise, if the body is riddled with tension and tightness caused from stress (it does this to protect itself), trying to meditate at this point can be quite uncomfortable. Why? Because there's too much tension within the body to allow the mind to slip into the neutral state. The body needs to be warmed up and loosened first. This is where complementary physical exercises can be really helpful.

The yogis knew this and it is why physical stretching and moving of the body (asanas), along with breathing exercises (pranayama), are such essential parts in reaching enlightenment (samadhi). I'm not suggesting you need to reach enlightenment here but if you are at the point where you can feel the heaviness and tension in your body from the stress and anxiety you've been exposed to, then my first recommendation is to not meditate but do what you can to release this tension from the body. Go for a run, have a stretch, do some deep breathing. Just shake out some of that anxious, bottled-up energy first. Even if you do this for just a couple of minutes, it can really help a lot with how comfortable and effective your meditation experience will be. For me, this usually consists of around five minutes of stretching before meditation, along with a quick deep breathing exercise. Once the body is feeling a bit of relief, the mind will find it easier to find some too.

The brain bicep curl

If you've tried meditation before, you will know that it can be pretty hard to stay connected to whatever you have decided is going to be your anchor point with the present moment. Whether that's your breath, a mantra, a bodily sensation, it doesn't matter, soon enough your mind will want to join the party and take over. Which is completely understandable considering that's what it's been told to do most of our lives. To think, question, plan, doubt. Whatever it needs to do to stay in control. It has often been considered a bad thing when we notice the mind stepping back into our headspace during meditation. We beat ourselves up that we've lost our focus and connection to the moment.

But there's a hidden benefit to what has just happened. Think about it. What has really happened? You've *noticed* the fact that your mind has entered into your space. In other words, you have become *aware* of this intrusion. It is a moment of *awareness* and that is the whole point of what we're trying to achieve here – developing our awareness. So instead of criticising yourself when this happens, celebrate it!

Another way I like to see this is the brain doing bicep curls. Each time you become *aware* that your mind has stepped in during meditation, treat this like another rep for the brain.

Here's what I mean: So you're meditating away, feeling connected to the present moment through your primary sense. Then, for some reason, your mind decides to ask the question, 'Am I actually doing this right?' For a moment, your mind has now slipped back into its thinking mode. Now, rather than starting a back-and-forth dialogue with this question – for example, 'I'm not sure. Am I doing it right?' – as this will keep you in the thinking mode and lead to frustration, just notice the fact the question has simply been asked and mark that awareness down as one brain bicep curl. Then shift your awareness back to connecting with the present moment. Continue to do this each time you notice a question, thought or your imagination stepping into your meditation. The more times you notice this, the more reps you're doing and the stronger your brain and level of awareness is becoming.

Grouping of small connected moments = a big plate of consciousness

A common misunderstanding about meditation is that it's meant to be this single pure stream of connected consciousness and that when this is broken, you aren't doing it right and should start again. This belief, especially when starting out, can obviously be quite frustrating and detrimental to whether you continue to practise meditation or not. Instead of trying to maintain this single stream of consciousness during your meditation, try simply looking for small moments of connection.

These might be just the tiniest, most subtle of things that you notice. The feeling of a cool breeze touching your skin. A single mantra expressed and felt. A tingling sensation at the tips of your fingers. All you're looking for is some type of connection with the here and now. Even if it's just for a few seconds, congratulations! Consider that meditation a success.

Now continue to do this over and over again, and group these small moments of connection together. Soon enough you'll find that you have experienced a big serving of yummy consciousness. This is the trick to meditation.

It is a moment of *awareness* and that is the whole point of what we're trying to achieve here – so instead of criticising yourself when your mind wanders, celebrate it!

Once you become more skilled and comfortable at finding these small moments of connection, you'll begin to notice that the breaks or interruptions in your connection with the present moment aren't as frequent. In other words, your moments of connected consciousness start to lengthen. This is you beginning to become stronger and more skilled at staying connected with the here and now.

What about all the distractions?

Another common challenge that comes up a lot during meditation is all the distractions that can happen when we're trying to practise. Motorbikes hooning past your window. Kids fighting in the next room. Your phone is ringing. Your pet is scratching around. And there you are amongst it, trying to get a little peace and a break from it all.

There're two answers to this challenge. The first is that meditation isn't necessarily an escape from reality, but an embracement of it. Yep, all the good and the bad. So far we've been using safe and familiar connection points to connect with the present moment (a physical sensation we notice in our body, a mantra, etc), but we can find this peace with connecting to anything in the present moment, even what we might deem a distraction. All those distractions are just other moments happening in the here and now and can therefore be used to connect to the present moment too. Yes, this might even include the noise of all the traffic outside your window. It might sound weird, but peace can be found in connecting with this 'distraction'. So when these 'distractions' happen, instead of trying to block them out, welcome them. Explore the distraction. What can you notice about it? The sounds, vibrations and effects it is having on and within you. Just observe and soon enough you'll notice that what was once a 'distraction' has now become a connection point to the present moment and is, oddly, quite peaceful.

The other option is that you can override these distractions through effortless repetition of another present moment anchor. The most effective of these is a mantra of some type. By simply repeating the mantra when these distractions are happening around you, the mantra is not allowing the distraction to grab your attention and take over. It acts like a rolling pin of sorts. By constantly 'rolling' out your mantra you are flattening out any distractions when they pop up. The more you 'roll it out', the calmer and smoother your brain chatter becomes. The key to this technique is that the repetition is effortless. It's not a 'do or die' focus and connection with the mantra. Just a carefree and effortless repetition.

We cannot stop life or what we might perceive as 'distractions' from happening. Nor is meditation a technique that somehow pauses things or gives you an escape from life (quite the opposite, actually). We can, though, learn to understand and learn from all aspects of life through the good and the bad, using meditation as the vehicle to do this. It can also be used to teach us how to effortlessly delight in life, showing us that there is no such thing as distractions in life, just other moments happening at the same time around us.

DEALING WITH DISTRACTIONS WHILE MEDITATING

Try this. Next time you're meditating and something distracts you, make the distraction itself your point of contact with the present moment. Even if it's just for a moment. Zoom into and connect with the distraction.

For example, if it's a motorbike hooning past your window, allow your awareness to go into this noise. What do you notice about it? Maybe how the sound starts off as a steady, chugging low volume that then amplifies quickly into more of a high, vibrating pitch. You can almost see in your mind's eye the motorbike rider turning their wrist on the throttle with the changing of this noise.

What you're doing here is making the distraction your point of connection with the present moment. This honing of awareness can take a little practice to get used to, but after a while you'll realise that peace can be found by connecting to anything that is happening within the present moment.

How long should I meditate for?

It's worth touching on this here as it's something I get asked a fair bit. My go-to response when I'm asked this question is, 'Any time is a good time to meditate.' Whether you can do 5, 15 or 50 minutes of meditation in a session, that's time well spent. When starting out, though, I would recommend doing several shorter meditations each day rather than trying to do one longer meditation. For example, start by doing two or three five-minute meditations a day. You could do one in the morning, one in the afternoon and another just before you go to bed, rather than attempting one 30-minute meditation in the morning. You can't expect yourself to run a marathon if you can't even run a couple of kilometres, and if you try to, you probably won't want to (or can't) run again for a while.

What's most important when starting out is that you're showing up each day and enjoying the process. Try to keep up this routine for about a month or until you feel ready

What's most important when starting out is that you're showing up each day and enjoying the process.

for a longer meditation. Then go to ten minutes and see how that feels. After a few weeks of that, try 15 minutes. The signal to look out for that will tell you that you've had enough is when you find it quite hard or frustrating to find and return to the present moment connection point. When the inner adventure turns into a feeling of being lost and confused, more than curiosity and wonder, it's time to stop and turn on the lights.

I find the sweet spot is being able work yourself up to do around 20 minutes of meditation comfortably. I do not think any more than this is really necessary most days. If you've been practising meditation for years and have the time and skill to do it for longer, go for it! When we get into healing types of meditation in Stage Two, these do require a little more time. But for now, and particularly for relief meditations, any time up to 20 minutes is fine – and let's be honest, finding an hour a day to sit in meditation is unrealistic for most of us.

How do I know when I'm meditating?

Seems like such a simple question, right? Yet when I googled this question I wasn't entirely impressed with the answers that popped up. Most of what I found were the outcomes of meditation, such as, 'I know I'm meditating when I feel less stress.' I don't think this answer really helps when you're sitting there with your eyes closed and asking yourself, 'Am I doing this right?'

The easiest way to tell whether you're meditating or not is when you're *feeling* and not thinking. This is meditation. You're *experiencing* the moment, is another way of putting it. So instead of 'Am I doing this right?', which is a thought, it's 'I can *feel* the cool air moving through my nostrils when I breathe in', which is a feeling. 'What is the smell of this rose?' is thinking. Experiencing the smell of the rose is feeling. Notice the difference. Meditation is the intentional act and experience of feeling and connecting with the present moment.

We often confuse these two, though, as thoughts can very quickly follow a feeling. For example, 'Gee that's a beautiful sunset' is a thought not a feeling. The feeling happened just before this. When you experienced the visual delight of the sunset.

Sometimes we also mistake thoughts for feelings. 'Gee my boss is annoying' is a thought that *triggers* the feeling of annoyance. But if we were to actually feel annoyance, what would it feel like? Maybe nausea in the stomach? Heat and tension along the forehead? Tightness in the throat? So when we look at what's causing our problems, it's not our feelings. It's our thoughts. They're either triggering us to feel a certain way or interrupting us from feeling a certain way. Meditation is training us to feel more and think less.

Meditation is training us to feel more and think less.

Do I need to sit still like a pretzel?

Just like mantras, the body positions for meditation have been developed and worked on for thousands of years by yogis, sages and mystics, so there's certainly a lot of merit to these postures. In saying this, no, you do not have to sit like a pretzel (traditionally referred to as the lotus or half lotus) in order to meditate. What's most important when it comes to your posture when meditating is listening to your body first and foremost – how you are feeling heading into your practice and what you require from the meditation.

For example, if it's just before bed and you are wanting to completely unwind and relax, sitting in an upright position to meditate doesn't make much sense. The body will be confused with what the mind is trying to achieve. So lie down on your back, rest your hands on your belly and have your head supported. This way the body and the mind are aligned with the purpose of the meditation. On the other hand, if you're starting out your day and would like to set it up feeling energised and focused, then sitting up nice and tall with your hands on your knees and palms facing up is telling the mind that 'I'm here and ready to tackle whatever comes at me.'

If you don't feel any of the things in the positions described in the meditation opposite, that's completely okay. The point here is to adjust and move different parts of your body into different positions that you feel are most appropriate for what you need at that moment, for example, relaxation, energy, focus, etc. There are hundreds of different hand positions you can play around with that provide different feelings. These are traditionally known as mudras. I'm sure you've seen one of the most common mudras used in meditation, thanks to all of the Buddha figurines in those trinket shops, where the hands are resting out on the knees, palms turned upwards and the index fingers are touching the thumbs. This is known as the gyana mudra, and is recommended for when you are using meditation to improve your focus and create a feeling of strength and power.

ALIGNING THE BODY WITH THE INTENTION OF YOUR MEDITATION

Let's do a quick little exercise to demonstrate this further. Take a moment to sit up nice and tall, as if there's a piece of string pulling you up from the crown of your head. Your legs don't have to be crossed, just however you're currently sitting. Let your shoulders drop down and back, away from your ears, so they feel like they are just hanging off your neck, and place your hands on your knees, with your palms facing upwards.

Now take a moment to see how the position feels. For me, this posture is quite vulnerable. I feel very open. As if I'm saying to the universe, 'Okay, give me what you've got.' I use this posture in meditation when I feel I need energy and guidance.

Now, keeping the same posture, turn your palms over so they are facing downwards on your knees. What difference do you notice? This simple movement of the hands turning over shifts my state from being quite vulnerable and open to a state of feeling quite grounded, stable and strong. I use this position when I feel I need certainty for a situation. Maybe an important meeting or decision I need to make.

Let's do one more. Rest one of your hands over the other in your lap just under your navel. Your two thumbs should naturally meet together at their tips. It doesn't matter which hand you place over the other, just whatever feels most comfortable for you. Now what signal is this position telling you? For me, this is a very safe and nurturing position. I use this when I might be feeling anxious or agitated. It gives me a sense that everything is okay and the security to work through things.

Coming out of heightened sensory experiences

What can often get overlooked, especially when you are engaging in some type of sensory exploration meditation, is the process of coming out of your meditation, when you are wrapping up your session. What tends to happen when we crack open our eyes and come back into 'reality' is that we just get straight back into life as per usual. Jumping up from our practice, grabbing our phones and seeing what we missed in the last 15 minutes or so. We rush back into our doing mode, without giving ourselves the deserved credit and acknowledgement for taking the time to appreciate our being mode. An extra minute or two of soaking up all the leftover residue from your meditation is highly recommended.

How do you do this?

It is important that you take a minute or two to do this when wrapping up your meditation, as it gives your mind and body an appropriate transition back into the 'real' world. It will also help you carry that calmness that comes with meditation into the rest of your day. Whereas if you were to just jump up and get straight back to work, treating your meditation as something that you've now ticked off your to-do list, you are allowing your thinking mind to take full control again straight away.

Even if you're short of time, it is better to finish up your meditation a couple of minutes earlier and go through this transition than rushing off straight after your practice. Allow yourself to experience all that leftover goodness for a minute or two. Let it all seep into your thoughts and actions after your meditation. Your usual self will thank you for it later when you're dealing with some type of problem or challenge.

COMING OUT OF YOUR MEDITATION

Once you've finished your meditation and you open your eyes, try to be as still as possible. Only let your eyes slowly move around and take in your visual surroundings. Observe all the colours, textures and movement happening around you. Notice how things might seem more vivid and obvious. This is because you've just taken yourself through an inner sensory journey and your senses will now be heightened. Take a minute to soak up all this new data. Simply sit there and enjoy it.

Then feel your breath for a moment and start to slowly move your limbs. Start with giving your toes a wriggle and rubbing your fingers together. Then do some big slow rolls of your shoulders and bending of your neck. A gentle twist of your lower back and a few nice deep breaths. Slow, intentional movements and stretches of your body.

Putting yourself into the eye of the storm

If you're really wanting to break free from the hold your mind has over you, to cure yourself from the conditioning you've been subjected to your whole life that has had you either constantly grasping for satisfaction or holding you down in comfortable complacency, we have to have to first give ourselves the needed space and relief to restore and balance our energy levels. Everything we've covered so far has been specifically for this purpose and to prepare you for the most common challenges you'll face when trying to do so. To get you comfortably into the eye of the storm. A calm space that provides you with some needed solace and put you in the best possible position, ready to take on Stage Two of our journey together.

My hope is that Stage One has given you the tools and insights to experience some relief from all the stress, tension and conflict you've copped over the years. Relief to finally take a breath and look around. Practise what we've covered so far for as long as you need to. Build yourself up and gather your strength and composure, because you're going to need it. It's now time to face the giant, dark storm that is swirling around and within us all.

Stage Two
HEALING

It is not the problem that is hurting you. It is your avoidance of it that is.

It was about 10 pm on just another Tuesday and there I was sitting on my bed just staring blankly at the wall. Completely numb and scared shitless. I had just walked away from a business I had invested so much time, effort and money into. Two weeks earlier, a ten-year relationship I was in had broken down and ended. My family, particularly my sister, were also going through an incredibly difficult time as we had just found out my brother-in-law had been diagnosed with stage three cancer (they had two kids at the time and he was just 32 years old.). I had also had a falling out with one of my closest friends. It would be safe to say that this was one of those 'breakdown moments' in my life.

When we encounter such difficult moments in our lives, most of the time we are able to turn to another source of support to help us navigate through it. Whether that's your partner, a family member, friend or colleague. Someone who can just provide that needed comfort. As I sat there on this night, though, I felt like I really didn't have anyone I could turn to. Sure, my family would have absolutely been there for me but, as I said, they were all dealing with and providing support (and rightly so) to my brother-in-law. My partner was no longer there. Neither was my best friend. I couldn't even distract myself with work because that was now gone too. It was just me, myself and the blank wall in front of me, and I was terrified.

I had been practising meditation for around four years leading up to that night. But I had only really used the practice as a tool to provide me with a bit of relief. Whether that was to destress after a long day of work or give me that extra bit of energy when I needed it. We've already spoken about the importance of this type of relief meditation and the steps required in order to experience it in Stage One.

I had read and heard about 'deeper' and more 'profound' spiritual experiences that people had during meditation but I'd always had a fairly sceptical outlook when it came to the more 'woo woo' side of meditation. 'Let the hippies have their fun with it, I've got work to do' was my general vibe around those meditation practices.

It was just me, myself and the blank wall in front of me, and I was terrified.

But here I was. All alone, full of fear and no idea what to do. So what does one do when they find themselves in such a situation? Turn on Netflix in the hope it all disappears. Honestly, that's what I did. I just wanted to distract myself for a while. I didn't have some enlightening meditation experience. I didn't even know that meditation could help me in this way at the time. I just turned on the TV in an attempt to just take my mind off my problems.

Call it a complete coincidence or a divine act of God, but when I turned on the TV this night there was a new documentary that had just been released called *Ram Dass, Going Home*. I had heard of Ram Dass a couple of times when talking about meditation with friends and colleagues. He was somewhat of a pioneer in bringing meditation from India to the West in the 1970s after getting fired from Harvard as a professor for experimenting with psychedelics. He wasn't someone I would have considered looking up to. I was more of a Steve Jobs kinda fan. But I certainly didn't have anything better to do. Well, at least I thought I didn't. So I pressed play and what transpired over the next half an hour would set in motion a journey of discovering how meditation can not only provide us with some relief, it can also truly change and rewire our lives completely.

Going to India

The documentary starts out with Ram Dass in the later stages of his life. Aged 87, he has had a stroke that has massively deteriorated his physical, verbal and cognitive functioning. I remember at one point when he is gingerly talking about his life since having the stroke, he whispers, 'I would not wish anyone a stroke but I would wish you the grace I have received from it. It has pushed me inside even more and it's so wonderful.' Then a huge smile stretches across his face and you can see the joy in his eyes. This remark fascinated me as I found it hard to understand how someone could genuinely see something like having a stroke as a blessing. He goes on to talk about how his relationship with death has changed through meditating. He says, 'When we contemplate death or pain regularly in meditation, it imbues this moment with added richness.'

These realisations he was sharing on tragedy, loss and pain began to put my own situation in perspective. It gave me that glimmer of hope that I could work this out on my own if I had to. As soon as the documentary finished, I downloaded his book *Be Here Now* (which I highly recommend) and stayed up the rest of the night reading it. About a third of the way into the book, when he gets to India, he talks a lot about spending time learning to meditate in a place up in the northern part of India near the Himalayas, called McLeod Ganj. I thought to myself, 'You've got to be kidding! There's a place where you can go to meditate and discover these profound things about yourself that has the same name as mine? Come on!' Another complete coincidence? Maybe, but it was enough for me. I booked a trip then and there to fly to India in two days' time.

I spent close to two months in India. Most of the time I was at a homestay with an Indian family up in the hills of McLeod Ganj. For the first week or so I just wandered around the little village like a confused, lost tourist. Popping into different temples, bookstores and cafes hoping a guru would magically appear and usher me into some secret hidden passageway that led to the promised land. The guru never came. But I did find two places that became the catalyst for this next phase of self-discovery I was about to go on.

The first was a place called Tushita, a meditation centre created for the study and practice of Buddhism from the Tibetan Mahayana tradition. The Dalai Lama is also a spiritual guide here so I thought there was bound to be some wisdom to be discovered. The other was a Vipassana meditation centre. I was really confused on my first couple of visits there as to why no one wanted to talk to or even acknowledge me. I soon came to realise that this was primarily a silent meditation retreat and most of the people there were taking part in one of these experiences.

As I partook in the daily meditations, workshops and courses that were being offered in these centres, along with doing my own sessions, reading and writing, the door into this deeper introspective world began to open. It started to become clearer how meditation could not only be used as a tool for relief when needed, but also as a type of portal to sorting out some of the more serious and deeper things in your life. How it can lead to fundamentally changing who you are. To heal yourself and change how you see, act and respond to the world around and within you. It's like you start to become this new person, or maybe a more accurate way to put it is, you begin to discover your true self.

Time to start digging

Don't worry, I'm not going to tell you that you have to go and wander around India for two months to start practising this type of meditation. I also really hope that you don't have to experience similar difficult moments to get to a point where this stage is essential. That's why I wrote this book: so we can open the door before tragedy comes knocking. To give you that needed bump out of your comfortable complacency bubble.

Something to note here too: trying to fast-track your way into this stage rarely works. Meaning, it is almost essential you spend enough time practising, enjoying and experimenting with relief forms of meditation first, which we've covered in Stage One. Your mind will need to be able to maintain a level of stability within the neutral gear before it takes on the swirling storm happening around and deeper within you. Once you're able to steady and calm the mind, you'll be in a much better position to handle what we're about to go through. So only if you're prepared and ready, let's continue …

Spooking yourself – here come the emotions!

I must admit that watching those 'spook' clips on social media is a guilty pleasure of mine. Where someone is hiding around a corner and then jumps out suddenly to scare their partner or friend. The look on their faces is always priceless. This is what can happen in meditation when you're finally getting the hang of it. When you're finally starting to experience and enjoy that sense of relief that meditating provides ... *Bang!* Out of nowhere this surging feeling of anxiousness begins to take over the body. This obviously comes as quite a shock and scares the hell out of most of us. When this happens we'll either just stop meditating because it's too uncomfortable or we'll allow the mind to come back in to take control and distract us from this feeling.

These 'spooky' moments are either memories of past experiences that have caused you pain, hurt and suffering, or current energy imbalances that are wanting to be settled, such as a grudge you're holding on to or a lie you're trying to conceal. They naturally arise when the mind finally settles and the body feels relaxed, safe and secure. It's like all the suppressed emotional sediment is finally able to float to the surface because you've finally learnt how to calm your mind down a bit.

You can only fully heal or deal with what arises when you're in this relaxed, calm state. Suppressed feelings need safety and space in order to be set free. You don't let go of a bull in a china shop. You wait until you're outside in a large, open paddock.

Suppressed feelings need safety and space in order to be set free. You don't let go of a bull in a china shop. You wait until you're outside in a large, open paddock.

Let the body know first

Our body is our vehicle designed to carry out the physical work we need to get done while we're alive and it's very good at doing what it's told. When it feels threatened, the body will do what it can to keep us safe. This is commonly referred to as activating the fight-or-flight mode. Do I stay here and prepare myself for battle? Or is it time to run and get the hell out of here? However, it can be easily tricked into acting a certain way. For example, whenever the brain experiences an uncomfortable feeling like anxiety or guilt, it sends out an alert signal to the body. Even if there is no immediate threat or danger, the body will still act as if there is because the brain has said so.

So when the brain experiences one of these 'spooky moments' during meditation, the body jumps in to try to protect itself. Tensing up your muscles, clenching your jaw, speeding up your breathing, pushing adrenaline through your veins. Pretty much the exact opposite of what you're wanting the body to do while meditating. Therefore, giving the body some assurance that everything is okay is needed first and foremost. We do this by overriding these reactions. Intentionally slowing down your breathing.

It's like all the suppressed emotional sediment is finally able to float to the surface because you've finally learnt how to calm your mind down.

Actively unclenching your jaw. Softening your muscles. Let the body know that it is still in a safe space and that the brain is just passing on a message as to what it thinks is happening. Continue to do this over and over again when 'the spooks' arise during meditation until you get to a point where you're casually acknowledging them. So instead of 'Argggggghh!! RUN!' it's 'Ah you're back … Welcome. What do you have for me this time?'

The campfire perspective

Have you ever sat around a campfire and just started gazing into it? Where you're just transfixed on it and this beautiful, calming feeling washes over you? Isn't it fascinating how watching something that can be so destructive as fire can also have such a soothing and calming effect on us? It's the same when we are able to get ourselves to a point where we can detach and observe those difficult emotions when they arise during meditation. If you've followed the steps so far in this book and taken your time to practise how to calm your mind by moving it into the neutral gear first, you should now be in a position to be able to try this exercise. Tread carefully, though, as this is where things tend to get quite tricky.

The easiest way I can explain what happens during this exercise is that instead of getting caught in the fire and letting it burn you up or running away from it altogether, you 'step out from the flames', take a seat and just watch the fire do its thing. Just like when you observed and connected with the present moment in Stage One for relief, you are now observing this emotional discomfort that has arisen either by chance or by invitation during your meditation. When we learn how to do this for long enough, the emotional discomfort shifts from experiencing it to witnessing it. This move is very liberating and, at the same time, quite intriguing. A calming sensation begins to wash over you as you sit and observe the different aspects of this once all-consuming emotional fire. You begin to notice the way it moves and flickers. How it changes in colour. How it affects its environment and how the environment also affects it. At first this is going to feel quite uncomfortable, as you've just stepped out from the flames and are still standing quite close to the fire. The hairs on your skin may still be getting singed. But at least now you're not fully engulfed by it anymore.

By learning how to just observe the emotional fire within, little by little, it will begin to dwindle of its own accord. Provided you keep a close eye on it to make sure no further fuel is added. Like thoughts of self-doubt and pity. These intrusive thoughts are like throwing gasoline onto the fire. It is quite amazing how by just observing something with intrigue and curiosity, it loses its power and control over you.

One of the most unhelpful things we can do at this point is ignoring and running away from the fire. Ignorance is like the wind. It will spread the fire further and quicker than anything else. Making it bigger and badder until it is all-consuming again.

Let's look at an example of where ignorance of emotional discomfort can lead. Say you've gone through a difficult break-up. Initially you have your friends and family to help you deal with the pain. But after a year or so has gone by, you've developed this strange, subtle feeling of anxiety. At first you don't think too much of it. You stay busy with your work and social life, ignoring what's going on inside you. But, little by little, this uneasy feeling gets stronger and stronger, especially when things are calm and quiet. Like when you're in bed at night. You use things like social media and alcohol to distract and suppress this feeling. This works for a while, but it still seems to keep coming back – each time with even more vengeance. You're not fully aware of it yet (notice the word *aware* here; it always seems to pop up when we talk about solving something) but this feeling is an unresolved emotion from your previous relationship.

Now, there're three destinations where this undealt-with emotion can end up. The first is you unconsciously add it onto your pile of insatiability. You use the anxiety as fuel to keep you busy in your pursuit for more. It keeps you in a frantic, unsatisfied state. The second option is, instead of it feeding your instability, you let the emotion engulf you. You become incognisant of it, numb from it. Accepting that this is 'just the way it is'. We know how detrimental both of these destinations can be, how they lead to an unaware life of unhappiness. The third option is you can choose to become aware of it and do something about it.

For you to do this, let me take you through an example of how I approach this type of difficult mental exercise in a way that's as practical as possible.

DEALING WITH EMOTIONAL DISTRESS

I first start with around 15 minutes of relief meditation. This allows me to feel calm and shift the mode of my mind into the neutral gear of observation. Then I will invite any emotional distress to arise.

Just another note of caution here: If you get to this stage of the meditation and it is too overwhelming, it may be due to deep-seated trauma experienced as a child or at any other point in your life. I recommend that you stop and see a clinical professional first, then possibly seek out a meditation guide who has extensive experience with this type of meditation to help you through a few sessions before trying it yourself. If it is uncomfortable but bearable, though, then you can continue with this exercise, but take your time and always remember, you are in a safe and supportive space when meditating.

Depending on how intense and extensive the emotional distress is when it arrives, this will determine how long I will observe and question it. This could be 5 minutes or 50 minutes. When starting out with this type of meditation, though, I wouldn't recommend adding any longer than 15 minutes on to your relief meditation; totalling no more than 30 minutes.

When the emotional distress arrives, whether by inviting it or it just organically appears and *spooks you*, keep first in mind what we spoke about with the body. As that'll be the first thing that will want to run or fight. Lengthen your breath and continue to actively release the tension in your body. You do NOT need to 'relieve' the pain or experience it again in your mind's eye. Just observe the associated form it has taken within you. Your subconscious will know what you are dealing with without having to paint the experience fully again.

Once you have noticed the associated form of emotional distress, observe where it is physically placing itself. Is it a feeling of nauseousness in the stomach region? Tightness in the chest? Constriction in the throat? Once you notice where it is, can you describe the shape of it? Is it moving? What colour is it? Remember that you're just observing all this. For me, a lot of the time it will either be black or red in colour, spiky and fairly solid in shape, and it can change in size depending on the level of seriousness of it. Its form could be completely different for you and it's important for you to try to describe how you see and feel it, however that may be.

Once you've seen the form of the distress for all that it is, you can change its elements to make it feel more comfortable for you. Shrink the size of it. Change the colour of it, the shape and weight of it. Do whatever you want to make it feel more comfortable. For me, I'll first shrink it in size. Then I'll change it to a more neutral, soft colour, like a light blue or a pale yellow. I'll also take the weight out of it and turn it into a mist type of form, rather than a solid form. The objective here is to change the nature of it however you like to make it more comfortable for yourself.

What do you want to do with the fire now?

Now that the fire is under control and you're feeling more comfortable with it, what do you want to do with it? Do you want to put it out completely? Watch it smoulder into nothing? Or maybe you want to gaze at it a little longer and see what it has to teach you? Maybe learn more about the effect the changing winds can have on it? Who or what adds fuel to it?

Let's use the example of the pain your ex may have caused you. Some questions you could now ask yourself while observing this emotional discomfort during meditation could be: Did my ex make me feel less than what I know I'm worth? Are there things I can admit and accept where I contributed to the break-up? Am I ready to let go of the weight this has over me? What do I need to do to really move on?

These are the types of questions I would encourage you to ask yourself when you reach the stage within your meditation practice where you feel safe and stable to do so. Whatever is causing the emotional discomfort, remove yourself from it first. Step out from the fire. Then look at it for as long as you need to and, when you're ready and feel comfortable, do with it as you wish, whether that be exploring how you can learn and grow from it, or let it go and move on altogether from it. This is how these first two stages of meditation work together. Experience the required relief first through observation. Then begin the healing through introspection.

How will you know what questions to ask yourself when you get to this point in your meditation?

Your intuition will let you know whether you're asking the right questions or not. For example, you might ask yourself, 'Am I ready and able to let go of this pain I feel?' You'll know whether you are or aren't ready yet and if not, ask something else. Maybe some questions that might help bring some clarity and perspective to your distress, like 'Why am I letting this affect me in this way?' and/or 'Is there something I need to learn from this pain? If so, what?' Just keep asking and exploring until you begin to find some answers. And you will, everything you need resides within. You will then feel the emotional distress losing its grip on you and you notice yourself becoming more comfortable and confident with the situation or issue and with yourself.

Once you feel like the weight has been dropped, take your time coming out of this type of meditation, as you'll

Your intuition will let you know whether you're asking the right questions or not.

most likely be quite sensitive and 'emotionally raw'. This is where the breath can be a wonderful companion. Take a few long, steady breaths when finishing up. Sometimes you might also feel the urge to cry. If you're in a space that you feel comfortable in doing so, just let it all out. Lastly, I find it helps to take a few further minutes to journal for a bit. Just get down on paper how you're feeling and anything else that comes to mind at this moment. This will support you and remove any further residue of the emotional weight you were holding on to.

After using this type of meditation to process a lot of your suppressed emotions that are causing stress and anxiety, you will begin to notice a shift in the type of person you are. Because a type of healing is taking place. For years it has probably felt like more and more cement has been constantly poured over you. Holding you down and keeping you stuck where you're at. This process we've just described and gone through begins to start chipping away chunks of this heavy weight. Bit by bit, freeing you up, and the more you practise this, the closer you will come to reclaiming your true self.

You're perfect

I know. That's a big call. Especially after everything we've just gone through. But because we've now started to strip back our outer layers, we will start to notice this light emerging through the cracks. So before things get too bright, I think now is the right time to drop this truth bomb. Underneath it all, you are perfect as you are in this very moment. Feels weird, right? Let me explain. Each soul that resides in every one of us, in its natural form, is perfect. It was perfect the day you were born and it will still be perfect until the day you die.

But before we get too carried away here and our ego starts patting itself on its back, first let's define what I mean by 'perfect'. Perfection is often misunderstood as something that is absolutely pure and right. This is not the true definition of perfection. Perfection comes from the Latin word *perfectio,* which actually means 'complete' or 'whole'. Another way of looking at something that is perfect is that it needs nothing. The soul requires nothing. Does that mean it wouldn't like to be uncovered and set free? No, not at all. It would love that. It just doesn't *need* it. Regardless of what you do in this life, your soul will always be there. Perfect as it is. Waiting patiently for you to let it shine ... or not. The choice is completely up to you. Either way, it is there residing within you at this very moment and it is perfect.

Nature is a wonderful example of this type of perfection. It does not need anything. It simply draws on everything that it has access to. Everything is already there for it to use or not. It is whole. Complete and perfect as it is. I love how even death brings about new life in nature. How the shadows of the world offer shade and needed refuge from the warmth and nutrients of the sun. The seemingly 'dark' works with the 'light' in harmony within its whole and perfect system. Our souls are the same. The soul has everything it needs at its fingertips. Yes, the soul carries pain, sorrow and grief. Along with happiness, peace and contentment. It's all there and it all serves a purpose. It is whole and perfect as it is within you at this very moment. Therefore, you must be perfect as you are in this moment as well.

What an incredible truth this is to know that in this very moment, however dark things may be in your life right now, or whatever has happened in your past, there is this essence residing within you, this very moment, that is, and will always be, perfect.

What about someone who is evil? Someone who has done and continues to intentionally do bad things. Surely, they can't be perfect? Well, let me ask you this. Were they born an evil person? No. They became an evil person through the exposure and conditioning of their environment. As hard as this is to say and acknowledge, underneath their calcified evilness is a flickering ember of perfection. A soul that is complete. That infant essence just waiting all the way deep, deep down inside to be found again. More often than not these people will never see this flickering ember of perfection, and maybe they don't deserve to. It still doesn't negate the fact that it's there, always was and will be.

Where I'm going with this is that at the core of who you are, your soul, your true self – call it what you want – however far down it is, however many layers have been stacked on top of it, it is there and it is perfect. What an incredible truth this is. To know that in this very moment, however dark things may be in your life right now, or whatever has happened in your past, that there is this essence residing within you, this very moment that is, and will always be, perfect.

Let's take this even a step further. Let's say that everything that means the most to you in this very moment is taken away from you. Your family, your friends, even all the material stuff you have and own like your home, your job and all of your money. It's all taken away from you this very moment. Yet in the place where you seem to have nothing, you are still perfect. That whole, complete seed of perfection within you is the only thing that will never leave you. Ever.

Our life's purpose is to find and return to this source of perfection within ourselves. Then gently nurture it so it grows and shines throughout every aspect of our lives. Everything that we've covered so far is doing just this – by using meditation as the vehicle to expose, accept and embrace this truth.

Building your new self

Now that we have been shown and unlocked this door to our true, whole selves, it is worth discussing some of the things to keep an eye out for at this stage. Just like the challenges you faced when going through Stage One there are obstacles that you will no doubt have to overcome during this stage too.

Watch out for your ego

When we begin to strip back these layers and free our selves, our ego will often try to seize this opening as an opportunity for recognition and control. Because our society has been built to reward progress, and you are now in a position to act and think with a greater level of freedom and awareness, the ego will sneakily try to claim a new position for itself in your 'new self'. I see it all the time in the wellness industry, religion and other spiritual constructs that can help liberate us. Once we've experienced this new taste of the truth, we fall back into following the same old pattern of pursuit and attainment that originally got us into this mess.

It is easy for us to fall for this as it is something we are very familiar with. A desire for wanting more. Continuing to progress and explore the deeper realms of your true self does not require a pursuit or desire for more, just a curious sense of genuine awareness. A continued interest in meditation and observing yourself without judgement and expectations. Only then will you be able to maintain that beautiful sense of freedom and peace of mind. Only then can the present moment unlock greater movements and realisations within.

You are your greatest therapist

Therapists, counsellors, psychologists, spiritual teachers – they all do wonderful work. The best of them, though, really just act as guides to help you discover and work through things yourself. But even then, their guidance still comes through their own filtered life experiences and learnt formulas. The old saying that 'no one knows you better than yourself' is true. It's just that we have to be very patient with ourselves and do a lot of digging to usually get to this realisation. If I'm being brutally honest, you don't even need this book. Everything that I've written about and suggested in here can be discovered yourself through your own self-observation and introspection – i.e. meditation. I think this is why the term 'go within and you'll find the answers' is so commonly used and suggested in spiritual texts. I believe this to be true. All the answers to your questions, pain and suffering can be found from within. We just need to calm the storm first, then ask what you are wanting to know, then quietly listen.

We can also be fooled into thinking that other people know better than us. They don't. I have now set up my very own internal filter and I would recommend you do the same. How this filter works is that every piece of advice I read or receive now, I run it straight through my filter. I ask myself, 'How does this genuinely sit with me?' If I'm not sure, I'll ask some further questions until the inner filter either confirms my reservations or accepts the advice. It doesn't matter how reputable, famous or rich the person is who is sharing what they know. Always run it through your own feelings first and then make up your own mind. This is also where the term 'trusting your gut' comes from. The more we can tune in to our feelings, the better we'll become at making decisions that are right and suited for ourselves.

In saying all of this, would we still benefit from genuine guidance and assistance when needed? Absolutely. Especially when we are either too lost to even know that we need help or are too broken to mend our own wounds. Sometimes advice or direction isn't even needed. Sometimes just a listening ear can heal the deepest of wounds that we were unable to fix ourselves.

This inner knowing also runs true when experiencing the present moment. You could try to describe the beautiful sunset that might be happening outside your window at this very moment to me. Being as precise and detailed as possible about it: the changing of colours, the feeling it is

It doesn't matter how reputable, famous or rich a person is who is sharing what they know, always run it through your own feelings first then make up your own mind.

evoking within you. This could paint a pleasant picture in my mind's eye. But it will never come close to what you are experiencing at this very moment. Words or paint on a piece of paper can do a great job of describing reality. But they will never be able to fully provide you with the true feeling itself. This is something you must experience for yourself. Everything you come across, observe and notice, the good, the bad and everything in between, is your experience. You are the artist who is in complete control of what you choose to see or not to see. This book, me and anyone else are just guides trying to shine a little light on the canvas.

This goes for the people closest to you, too. If you really want to touch and immerse yourself in reality and truth, you have to do this by yourself. Any outside influence will contaminate the moment. This doesn't mean you don't listen to them or appreciate their perspective and support when it's given. Let your new developed level of awareness take on their words and then run them through your own feelings filter. Does it sit right with you? If the answer is yes, great! Give thanks. If it doesn't, great! What have you learnt? As William Ernest Henley wrote in his poem, 'Invictus': *I am the master of my fate, I am the captain of my soul.*

Feeling the love

Take a look around outside. Does nature ask anything of you? Does it favour certain people and not others? No. A tree will offer its shade to anyone walking past it, regardless of their character, history and reputation. A rose does not require you to smell its fragrance in order for it to feel loved. Truly beautiful things do not seek attention. You want to know what real love looks like? Observe the nature of nature. Notice how it does not ask for anything or discriminate. It does not need to do anything to feel complete and loved. There is nothing you need to do either to feel this way. There are only things you need to let go of.

Now that we are able to create a safe simulation space within our meditation practice to heal and rewire our inner world, here is a concept to contemplate about the most powerful feeling of all. Love. This will help you be able to let go of the things that might be shrouding your ability to truly love and be loved.

A principle we have developed over time and now use to maintain control over ourselves and other people is the 'reward for effort' principle. Throughout our whole lives we have been told and trained that the more effort, energy, time and money we put into something, the more we should expect in return. Behave, and you'll get a treat. Work harder, and you'll get a promotion. How many times have you heard, 'What's my ROI (return on investment) with this?' Almost everything we do now in our day-to-day lives has some element of 'what do I get out of this?' to it. This principle is closely related to the natural law of 'cause and effect' but there is one very important difference between the two of them – expectation.

The natural law of 'cause and effect' does not expect anything in return for its effort. The tree doesn't expect you to repay the favour of providing you shade. It gives it to you freely expecting nothing in return. It does this for no other reason than because that is what it is.

There is something truly beautiful, and powerful, when you receive love from someone and they sincerely don't expect anything in return. No recognition. No act of love needs to be given back. It is just given to you completely and freely. We almost don't know how to react when this happens because it is so unusual to experience these days. Even something which might seem to be a very charitable act still almost always comes with a sliver of hidden expectation tied to it. Waiting for just a simple 'thank you'

The natural law of 'cause and effect' does not expect anything in return for its effort.

in return is proof of this. It mightn't seem like much but there's still this slight expected 'reward for effort' present.

Using meditation to practise this type of unconditional love without expecting anything in return is a great way to start rewiring the perspective of love that we have become so accustomed to. It is a fascinating thought that the greatest act of love you can do is not of selfless service but your own contemplation of love itself. To do this, you will have to first come to a point with your Stage Two meditation practice where you've processed and dealt with most of your own emotional blockages. Otherwise they will block you from even trying to engage in this type of practice.

REWIRING EMOTIONS THROUGH UNCONDITIONAL LOVE

Begin your meditation as per usual until you can sit comfortably and calmly without any prominent emotions arising. Then bring someone into your mind's eye who you *don't* like that much. Paint in the details of this person until they become quite clear. You might organically start to feel tension or uncomfortable doing this, but continue to relax your body and breathe calmly as you're bringing this person to your mind's eye. Once you have a clear picture of them, begin to share unconditional love with them. There is no hidden agenda to your efforts with this. Start with just small, genuine expressions of unconditional love, such as a warm smile. Even if their response is one of annoyance or disregard, keep expressing small amounts of unconditional love to them. You aren't expecting anything in return. Just freely giving these small expressions of unconditional love to this person.

Now shift your awareness back to connecting with something in the present moment. Maybe your breath or the feeling of the sun on your face. Just come back to connect with something in the here and now. The experience, thought and visual of the person who you were giving unconditional love to is now completely gone. You are just simply connecting with the present moment again via one of your senses. Do this for around five minutes or so and then begin to slowly come back into the thinking world. Similar to coming out of a healing meditation, you may be feeling quite sensitive and emotionally raw at the end of this meditation. So take your time and again, use your breath as a wonderful companion to stabilise your emotional state and journal a bit to solidify and process and remaining emotional residue.

What you have just done in that meditation is a process of rewiring what love is all about. Love born from awareness. Practise this type of meditation regularly until you find yourself acting this way in your day-to-day life. Genuinely giving without expecting anything in return is truly one of life's purest experiences.

A small word of caution when you begin to bring this into your everyday life. Unfortunately, some people will take advantage of your unconditional love. Most people aren't used to this type of love and will therefore begin to grasp for it and use it for themselves to fill their own void of lovelessness. Don't worry, they don't know any better. As your awareness continues to expand the more you meditate, you will be able to identify these types of people fairly quickly. You can try to explain what you have learnt and how they, too, can experience this type of love as well themselves, without anyone or anything else. However, if they are not at a point in their lives to understand this, give them unconditional love anyway and then let go. You have shown them what is possible and this is enough. Let them witness this and encourage them to explore with their own curiosity to discover this beautiful realisation for themselves.

Emotion-less not emotionless

After you have practised Stage Two types of meditation for a while and have begun to become more comfortable and skilled at detaching yourself from your inner turbulence, you will find yourself not getting caught up in the usual day-to-day dramas. You might start noticing how certain situations or people don't affect you as much. This change in behaviour can often be initially criticised by those around you as they are used to you reacting in a certain way. Comments like 'What's wrong with you?' or 'What's gotten into you?' can be received as other people are now confused, possibly even let down, by your new emotion-less response.

Being emotion-less in not a bad thing. It doesn't mean you don't feel anything. In fact, you will feel more of your feelings after you've been practising meditation for a while. You just aren't getting as emotionally caught up in them as much as you used to. You have developed the skills of observation, detachment and introspection. This is a big sign that your self-awareness is progressing.

You can notice these qualities in great leaders and people who have been meditating for some time. When everyone around them is 'freaking out' about something and getting overwhelmed by their emotions, this person still seems to be calm and composed. It's not that they can't feel what's going on, they have just learnt how to observe, detach and respond differently to situations that most people find stressful.

Unfortunately, being emotional is often celebrated in society. It can be a source of entertainment. Gossip around the water cooler at work can be alluring. Because emotions elicit emotions. So when someone is being emotional, it triggers others to feel their own emotions too and feeling something is better than feeling nothing. We feel included. So we celebrate emotional people because it evokes emotions within ourselves.

Being emotional can also be mistaken for being vulnerable and sharing your feelings. Which again is often rewarded in society with sympathy in return. Of course, if you've been holding on to something and get emotional when you finally release it, this is totally understandable. I just wanted to make the point that we can still be vulnerable and share our feelings without becoming emotional. People at first may find this type of response odd, because you are sharing something that is personal and difficult to share but don't seem emotional about it. Over time, though, this skill of detaching yourself from your emotions when sharing something personal will become a quality of strength that people will be attracted to and find comfort in.

This skill is also very handy when dealing with conflict in the moment. I remember one such occasion when my now wife and I had just moved into a new apartment. We were both very excited as the place had beautiful harbour views and was close to some of our good friends. After we had finally moved all our things in, we were cleaning up everything and we put a wooden box filled with folded-down cardboard boxes into the recycling bin. The next day when I woke up and stepped outside to go to work, I noticed that the box we had put in the recycling bin was now on the roof of our car. At first I thought that my wife for some reason had taken it out and left it there by accident. I went back up the stairs and asked her if this was the case, to which she gave me a look of complete bewilderment. So now we were both wondering why someone would take the box out of the bin and put it on the top of our car.

When we were moving our things in, we met a nice woman who lived on the floor below us. She welcomed us to the building and said that if we needed anything to just

Over time, the skill of detaching yourself from your emotions when sharing something personal will become a quality of strength that people will be attracted to and find comfort in.

come and see her. I certainly didn't think I would go to her for some help so soon. I knocked on her door, she opened it and I began to explain what had just happened. She knew straight away.

'That would have been one of the neighbours,' she said. 'How do I say this … she can be difficult to deal with.'

I thanked her but on the inside I was thinking, 'Great, we've just moved into this place and have now found out that one of our neighbours is the type of person who would take rubbish out of the bin and put it on the top of our car.' How was I going to handle this? My old self would have taken one of two options: a) Let it slide, convincing myself that I made a mistake and then trying to avoid crossing paths with this person as much as possible to limit any potential conflict with them in the future; or b) Confront them, put them in their place and make them realise that this type of behaviour isn't acceptable.

I know that because of my meditation practice teaching me how to detach myself from my own emotional reactions that can arise within Stage Two–type meditation, I was able to pull myself up and out of the situation without getting overly emotional. I was able to ask myself why this person may have done something like this. When we learn to see things from this perspective it soon becomes obvious that someone like this is hurting themselves. They have allowed their emotions to get the better of themselves and have now acted out.

With this understanding, I went and knocked on her door and waited patiently for her to answer. As the door slowly opened, I could sense she was ready to get into a verbal battle. I started off with, 'Hi, my name's Luke. We just moved in near you.' There wasn't much of a response, just a grunt of acknowledgement. 'Anyway,' I continued, 'did you put that box that we put in the recycling bin on top of our car?'

Her eyes widened as if she had been given an opportunity to strike. 'You can't put wood in the recycling bin!' she yelled at me.

'Sorry about that,' I replied calmly. 'We honestly didn't know that.' (Which was the truth. We thought wood could be recycled.) I then continued, 'If there's anything else like this that bothers you, please just come and chat with us and let us know.' To which she didn't know how to respond.

Most people like this are used to emotional responses to their actions. They are expecting to either go into battle or have the other person cower away. When someone is calm and reasonable with them, they don't know what to do. With a confused look on her face, she stuttered, 'Ah, ah, ah, okay. Thank you. Will do.' Then she closed the door.

From that day on she was nice to us. All the other neighbours were shocked. 'What did you do?' they all asked. 'I just went and had a chat with her,' I replied.

That's what meditation can bring into your everyday life. The ability to not get caught up in all the emotional games we often play within ourselves and with other people. It brings you to a point where you're able to 'just have a chat' in a very calm and reasonable manner. This skill will serve you very well throughout your life.

Catching yourself in the moment

So far we have predominantly discussed how we can use meditation to help us sort out our inner world. But it's all well and good to be able to process all of this difficult emotional stuff when we're by ourselves in a room with our eyes closed – what about when we're out and about in the outside world? What about when we're in the moment dealing with a stressful situation or person we've encountered during the day? I hear you.

The story of my neighbour in the previous section shows how dealing with emotions in meditation can help us in our everyday lives. Here are some further differences I've noticed in my day-to-day life that have carried over from meditating regularly, plus a little mindfulness game I like to play that has also helped me when I've found myself in a stressful situation.

First, the most immediate change I noticed when I started meditating was how I wasn't getting as distracted as much during my work day as I was before. I was able to focus for longer periods of time without the urge of wanting to pick up my phone or shift my attention to some other task. This is a natural bonus side-effect of practising

Stage One types of meditation. As not only does this style of practice provide relief to the thinking mind by moving it into the neutral gear, it also improves your ability to focus. This happens because you are consistently directing your awareness back to a single connection point with the present moment throughout your meditation. In other words, you are also training your mind to focus on one thing for an extended period of time.

The second key difference I began to notice, particularly after I started practising Stage Two types of meditation, was that I wasn't emotionally reacting as much to certain situations or conversations that would usually trigger a feeling of stress, anxiety and/or frustration in me. I found myself calmer in these moments, such as the situation with my neighbour. This outcome is often spoken about as a benefit of meditation but why this happens rarely gets shared. What's important to note here is that if you only practise Stage One types of meditation, I don't think you will experience this particular benefit as much. Stage One meditations are more likely to provide emotional relief when needed, not emotional regulation in the heat of the moment.

Stage Two types of meditation, however, as we've recently gone through, help us observe and process emotions. This is also very helpful in preparing us for when difficult situations arise in real-time, as it is also working as an emotional simulator of sorts. Just like when a pilot steps into a flight simulator to practise dealing with sudden, difficult situations, so that if anything similar happens when they are actually flying, they are prepared to deal with it and the more they practise in the simulator, the more they are training their auto-response system in their subconscious.

So instead of emotionally reacting or suppressing our emotions when difficult situations arise in everyday life, our newly developed level of awareness automatically kicks into gear to help us out. Your subconscious says, 'Ah, we've been through something like this before. I know how to handle this.' Then it automatically begins to initiate the process of observing all the elements that are involved for what they are and not letting the emotional weight they carry with them overtake you. Pulling you up and out of the fire to see everything from a bird's-eye view. This is how your practice done in your meditation simulator will help you tremendously in dealing with day-to-day difficulties when they arise.

So instead of emotionally reacting or suppressing our emotions when difficult situations arise in everyday life, our newly developed level of awareness automatically kicks into gear to help us out.

Catching yourself

The mindfulness game I like to play that can also assist in dealing with the everyday challenges is called 'catching yourself'. Even when we are meditating a lot, there are still going to be times when we get emotional and caught up in the moment. So now I try to 'catch myself' and notice when a situation has evoked an emotional response in me and has taken over my state of mind.

Now, when I notice myself in these emotional states, I can't help but laugh a little and shake my head at myself. 'I can't believe you've fallen for this again, Luke,' I say to myself. I then take a deep breath and allow my awareness to zoom out from the situation to gain some perspective of everything that's going on. This act of 'catching yourself' in the moment becomes easier and easier the more you meditate because it is very similar to when you are actually meditating and you catch yourself wandering away from your connection with the present moment.

Positive thinking vs meditation

Positive thinking and meditation often get lumped together. But they are quite different. Although positive thinking can be helpful to some degree when dealing with difficult emotions, it does not fundamentally deal with the root cause of what's really going on. It just overwrites it for a very short period of time. You can see this when someone says they're really into 'positive thinking' but they look as if they are trying to keep up this type of facade. A false hope of sorts. 'Just stay positive and everything will be fine,' they say to themselves as they run around with this frantic look in their eyes. I just want to stop them and say, 'No, I'm sorry, but it won't be fine if you keep this up.' Again, though, this usually isn't their fault. They don't know anything better and positive thinking does do a good job of masking emotional pain.

It doesn't matter how many positive affirmations you say to yourself, you can't trick yourself into healing. True healing requires a process of dealing with what caused the pain directly. A process that first provides you with a safe, calm space in order for you to observe, understand and then deal with the cause directly – this is what relief meditation will do first and foremost (which is covered in Stage One) and then healing meditation will deliver, as we've discussed in this section.

It doesn't matter how many positive affirmations you say to yourself, you can't trick yourself into healing.

Manifestation vs meditation

I'm sorry to say this but manifestation isn't meditation either. Like positive thinking, it does have its benefits. It can help with providing clarity on your goals and aspirations but, again, it is usually used as a mask to hide the truth. It won't help you cure your insatiability or incognisance either, unfortunately. If anything, it tends to confuse these two symptoms. It can bring a sense of delusion to your incognisance – for example, 'If I just act as if it will all come true, it will.' Or it can become a fuel for your insatiability – for example, 'What next do I need in my life? I will manifest it into my world!'

So why are positive thinking and manifestation so popular and commonly associated with meditation? Because they are both mental exercises like meditation and can provide a similar, yet fake, feeling to meditation.

Meditation uses the present moment as a portal to your inner workings. Whereas positive thinking and manifestation use the thinking mode of the mind as a vehicle to try and bring something external inwards to solve a problem, which just creates more traffic and confusion in the mind.

Meditation uses the present moment as a portal to your inner workings.

What about gratitude?

Ah, now we're talking! Gratitude and meditation are the best of friends. The big difference between gratitude and the two mental exercises on page 208 is that gratitude is all about what is, rather than what you want or what you're trying to convince yourself of. It is the truth. That is why it goes so well with meditation, because meditation is the process of tapping into what is here and now, and gratitude is the process of being thankful for what is here and now. A match made in heaven. Gratitude is the love and appreciation of what is. In other words, it's 'loving awareness'.

What's also interesting is that when meditation and gratitude combine, they actually deliver what most people try to use positive thinking and manifestation for. Firstly, there is not a more positive and pleasant feeling for the mind than when it is connected with the present moment. Think of your favourite memories. All of them happened when you were fully absorbed in the moment, with all your senses connected and buzzing. If you want to feel more positive, move yourself into the present moment more often.

And then the trick to manifesting what you want in your life is actually being grateful for what you already have. For example, say you are really wanting a partner in your life. If you were to follow the traditional guidelines to manifest this into your life, the mental exercise may go something along the lines of, 'My dream partner is coming to me right now.' Now what has this type of statement created? It has created an expectation. Whenever you hold an expectation in the mind, this creates an equal associated amount of stress and/or anxiety with it. Will it happen or won't it happen? The longer this expectation is there, the greater the pressure it will have on you. You can try to cover this up with more affirmations and manifesting but eventually if it doesn't come to fruition, it will start to seep through your character as either desperation or disappointment. 'Why hasn't my dream partner come along yet?' you're left saying to yourself.

Instead, try taking some time during your meditation to give thanks for the wonderful relationships you currently have in your life. This could be with your close friends or family, anyone you feel currently thankful for in your life. When you do this, what feeling does it create within you? This creates love. Pure love. There are no expectations, no weight, no stress. Just a feeling of love. Now who would you be more attracted to, someone who is showing signs of disappointment and desperation or someone who is filled with self-confidence and love? This is how you 'manifest' your ideal partner, or anything else for that matter, into your life – giving thanks for what you already have.

If you want to feel more positive, move yourself into the present moment more often.

Supercharging your gratitude

Bringing gratitude into meditation is a wonderful idea. As highlighted in the previous section, it can be used in your practice to 'manifest' what you feel like you're missing in your life. It can also be used as a wonderful finisher to any meditation as well, especially a Stage Two–type meditation. This is because you have just taken yourself through a process that can be quite confronting (dealing with difficult emotions). After going through this, shifting your focus to someone or something you are grateful for will instantly bring about a positive state of mind and balance your emotional scales.

To supercharge this exercise, there's a powerful three-letter word that will take the effects you feel from gratitude to a whole new level:

WHY

Why are you grateful for this person or thing? Most of the time when we engage in some type of gratitude exercise, whether it's writing down what you're grateful for or thinking of someone you're grateful for during a meditation, we are just bringing to mind a surface level feeling of this gratitude. This is still beneficial but in order for you to really experience and appreciate what you are grateful for, ask yourself and contemplate *why* you are grateful for this person or thing. This makes your gratitude a whole lot more real and meaningful.

Let's say, for example, you bring to mind how grateful you are for your dad. Rather than just stating this, contemplate why you are grateful for him too. What happens when you do this? You go deeper into your feelings. You're not just grateful for your dad. You're grateful for him *because* he makes you feel safe. *Because* he's always there and will always be there for you. See how the 'why' takes it to a whole new level? The 'why' is always more powerful than the 'what'.

SUPERCHARGING GRATITUDE

To put this into practice, simply add this supercharged gratitude exercise after you have taken yourself through a Stage Two type of meditation. Keeping your eyes closed, invite someone or something into your mind's eye that you're grateful for. Then, for a few minutes, just contemplate why you are grateful for them/it. Let yourself feel these reasons why. Notice what effect they have throughout your body and state of mind. Do this for however long you like or until you feel more balanced in your emotional energy levels. Finish your practice with three deep breaths and a final 'thank you' to all that is and all that will be. This is a wonderful way to wrap up a Stage Two type of meditation.

Spirituality and meditation

Spirituality and meditation are often spoken about in the same sentence. Some would even consider that one is synonymous with the other. I have, however, intentionally tried not to bring spirituality into the mix too much with what we've gone through so far. Mainly because I don't believe you have to be spiritual to practise and receive most of the benefits of meditation. The more you practise, though, the more you'll probably start to feel things that are hard to explain.

The two are often associated with each other because meditation usually leads people to act in what most would consider a more spiritual manner. You might find yourself becoming more empathic, understanding and patient. But I wouldn't consider these to be signs of only a spiritual person. I would consider them signs of any good, strong and capable person.

Some people try to use meditation to experience some type of spiritual awakening. This pursuit will only result in either disappointment or a false belief. Spirituality is not some type of achievement. It is a blessing. A blessing that comes about through awareness. It is you becoming aware of everything about yourself and the gift of life. There is nothing more spiritual than this.

All you need to do is observe the natural world, starting with yourself, with a deep sense of curiosity and this blessing will reveal itself to you. I think this is what Jesus meant when he said, 'Behold, the kingdom of God is within you.' Study your emotions and reactions, both positive and negative, without any judgement, preaching or even intention to change them. Just witness them. Doing this throughout your life will bring you closer in contact with spirituality than any other practice, process or religious beliefs.

The awakening of living an aware life

By going on this journey together so far and really giving everything we've covered a 'red hot crack', my hope is that you have firstly experienced some relief from the trap our minds can hold over us. The second thing I hope you've experienced is that you've also now been able to clear some of the emotional weight that may have been holding you back from being your true, best self.

While all this has been happening, there has also been something wonderful developing underneath it. Your awareness. Bit by bit, it has slowly been expanding. With each meditation you have done, with each concept you have contemplated, your level of awareness has also developed that little bit more. Just like every time you go to the gym or for a walk outside, you are taking one more step to improving your health.

You mightn't necessarily see the transformation physically as your awareness expands initially, but it is most definitely happening. This new way of being starts to open up a new way of living. A life that is full of joy and genuine happiness. A life without suffering and oppression. A life of awe and wonder. A life to be truly treasured and rejoiced.

Stage Three
HAPPINESS

There is no greater happiness
we can experience than allowing
ourselves to fully be immersed
in and completely connected with
life itself.

Tears were streaming down my face. It was a Friday morning and I was just doing my usual morning meditation. There was nothing different about it. I wasn't trying out some new-fangled meditation technique. Nothing was different about me either. I wasn't in any emotional distress, nor had I received any amazing news that had put me in a good mood. It was just another standard Friday morning. But what was happening in that moment was far from standard.

It is difficult to describe what was going on. The word that comes to mind when I talk about this experience is 'oneness'. Where the *me* melted into *the everything*. There was this type of vibration pulsing throughout my entire body. I felt completely connected. Plugged into life itself. And with this feeling came a deep appreciation and understanding of the union of all things.

To be honest, I don't like talking about this experience with other people. I find it has this *wanting* effect on those listening. It arouses a type of desire to experience something similar, a request for a fast-track to the same destination, a hack of some type. A response of, 'Just tell me how I can experience it too.' But I'm sorry, this isn't something you can google. I know this will sound uninspiring but it is something that will happen when it happens.

What I do know for sure is that if you have taken the time to follow and put into action the steps we have laid out so far, then you have set yourself up as best as possible to experience something similar. I can't give you an exact date as to when something like this could happen. It could be after a few weeks of going on this journey or after a few years. Maybe even never at all. What's most important is that you let go of wanting this experience to happen. Just like what I've recommended multiple times when practising meditation itself. Let go of what you are wanting to happen and simply allow yourself to just experience what is. Trust the present moment. It will never let you down.

The last stage of our journey together is a celebration. As you so rightly deserve. You've been through a lot so far and now it's time to party! This is also what life truly wants for you more than anything. To squeeze as much as possible from it. To walk through each and every day in awe. Full of love and gratitude. But this doesn't mean you're wandering around aimlessly with rose-coloured glasses on, immune to any negativity or painful experiences. It means that you've finally found and understand what life is all about. You finally become aware of this precious gift we've all been given. The good and the bad and why it is necessary for us to go through all the highs and lows and everything in between. So go and grab a glass of bubbly if you want. Because it's time to rejoice and celebrate you and your life!

Our life's purpose

I spent a lot of my life wondering what the purpose of it was. Trying to figure out what I was meant to do. Why am I here? I read countless personal development books on 'discovering your life's purpose' and tried everything. All of which still left me feeling subtly unsatisfied. Until I experienced this surreal moment of connection that Friday morning. What I finally came to realise after that moment is that we all have the same purpose in life, which is:

To experience life as much as possible.

That is it. Our purpose is not to work out what we are here to do, but to experience who we are. Make this your primary goal in life and everything will make sense. What you are meant to do, contribute, give and receive will become clear if you make experiencing your life your primary purpose.

But how and why does this work?

Our purpose is not to work out what we are here to do, but to experience who we are.

When we begin experiencing life more, rather than thinking about it, our awareness increases. We become more aware of what feels right and what doesn't. What we're good at and what we're not. What is hurting and keeping us less than what we truly are, and what makes us feel alive and fulfilled. Awareness shines a light on our own insecurities and habits of self-sabotage. It exposes the intentions of those around us and leads us to making choices that are more aligned with who we truly are and not what we, or anyone else, *thinks* we should be.

However, we have to train ourselves to experience more. Even though experiencing is our most natural state of being, almost everything around us has conditioned us to stay confined within the thinking mode of our minds. Thinking should be used as an asset to enhance our experience of life, not control our way of living, and meditation is one of the few exercises that trains us to experience life more through observation, introspection and, now, celebration.

Expanding our sensory experience

As you know and have experimented with over the course of this book, we've all been given five key senses to experience life: sight, hearing, taste, touch and smell. Unfortunately, most of our waking lives are spent in auto-pilot mode, where these senses are operating at their BAM (bare ass minimum) to get us through life. We have already explored how engaging our senses in different ways can lead to some big breakthroughs. In Stage One, we used our senses in a narrowing manner to isolate and connect with the present moment. This was necessary for us to be able to establish a state of calmness and stillness within the mind first. We then engaged the same senses in a different way to help us heal and rediscover our true selves through observing and processing emotional blockages. We are now going to call upon them once again to help us in this last stage of experiencing life to the fullest.

This is where the term 'mindfulness' joins the party. Mindfulness is the state when we are experiencing all the richness and joy that life has on offer. In other words, it is when we/our minds are living life to the *fullest*.

It will seem almost impossible to live a mindful life if you haven't first given yourself the appropriate time and space to learn how to calm the mind (Stage One) and have processed most of the emotional distress that has been holding you down (Stage Two). Once we have gone through these pivotal stages, it will become a lot easier to practise and embrace this new, mindful way of living. This is because you now have the ability and skill to experience the moment without feeling frazzled and/or being weighed down by emotional distress.

This mindful way of living will naturally start to unfold as you emerge from these stages. You will begin to notice and celebrate more of the everyday that is happening around and within you. This is where the real richness of life is found. When the ordinary starts to become extraordinary. Unlike when we are learning how to move the mind into the neutral gear which requires a narrowing of our senses, we are now ready and at the stage to *expand* and open up our senses with curious and intentional awareness. We do this by introducing certain new types of meditations and mindful exercises that will take these everyday experiences and feelings of joy and connection to an even deeper and more meaningful place. Are you excited to explore this realm? Me too. Let's do it!

Your free ticket to the greatest show of all

The more aware you become of yourself and your environment, the more eager your soul will become in wanting to show you how life can *really* be lived and experienced. It's like you've stumbled upon a secret passageway in your very own backyard that leads you into this new fascinating and vivid world, full of stunning scenery, nature and landscapes. At first this newfound freedom from within can be quite overwhelming and exciting. Therefore, before you go bounding off into this newfound wonderland we need to to make sure the ego doesn't seize this opportunity to gain control. We do this by channelling this exciting surge from within through meditation. It will show you how to handle and maintain this exciting new stage of your life, without the ego taking over and sending you down a path of false fulfilment.

DELIGHTING IN SENSORY EXPANSION

To start adding this to your meditation practice, begin as per usual with relaxing the body and getting the mind into the neutral gear (this should now take you around ten minutes or so). Once you are feeling settled and safe, this time, instead of either continuing to focus your awareness on a single connection point or inviting emotions to arise to be processed and dealt with, allow your senses to actually open up and expand. For example, if you are using your breath as an anchor to the present moment, shift your awareness to your hearing sense and see if you can begin to simply welcome all the sounds that are happening around you in that very moment.

At first, this might feel quite unusual and overwhelming, as up until this point we have either used meditation in a manner to narrow our awareness or process emotions. Just be patient and really try to simply have some fun with this transition. Continue to allow your hearing sense to expand further and further, floating from one noise to another. Start off with whatever the most obvious sound you hear in that moment. This could even be what you would have previously considered to be a distraction, like the sound of a car moving past your window or some chatter from the TV that's on in the next room. Whatever it is, just let your hearing sense soak it all up. As if you are listening not just with your ears, but your whole body. Feeling the sounds without trying to control or block anything. Just pure observation. If another sound suddenly comes into your range of listening, allow your awareness to go and explore that while it is present. What do you notice about that noise? The tone, the volume? Again, just take it all in. It's like your hearing sense is a part of a contemporary dance. Moving gracefully from one sound to another and you're in the front row just witnessing this beautiful performance play out in front of you.

Once you feel comfortable observing your hearing sense perform, you can then invite your other senses to join the show. The most common sense to join in next is the visual sense. The visual sense brings form and colour to your hearing sense's performance. For example, you might begin to notice shapes and colours form in your mind's eye that marry with the sounds you are hearing. The sound of that car passing by your window could bring a visual into your mind's eye of a tyre pressing into the bitumen or it could just be a moving colour of some sort heading in the same direction that the sound is going. The key thing to do here, whether the visual arrived of its own accord or you invited it, is to once again just sit back and enjoy the show.

The other main sense I would encourage you to explore when doing this type of meditation is your physical feeling sense. Especially when meditating outside and you are exposed to the wonders of nature. This could be allowing your awareness to feel the cool breeze brushing through your hair or experiencing the warmth of the sun touching your bare skin. Opening up this sense to feel your environment can be a beautiful experience and also begin to foster that sensation of oneness with everything. The understanding that your physical self is connected with the atmosphere at all times. Which is also then connected to everything else around you as well. There's you and what you can see, which could be the sun itself or the coffee mug on your table, and there's the air in between connecting it all together. A complete union and harmony happening at each and every moment. Nothing stands alone in this world.

What will most certainly happen as you are noticing all your senses perform is a reaction within your body to all of this. This is just the soul delighting itself in experiencing life. This usually comes in waves of tingling sensations or vibrations throughout the entire body, or maybe a feeling of weightlessness or a floating sensation. And it's almost always accompanied with some tears of joy and happiness. When these reactions happen, try to simply allow your awareness to bask in the magic and wonder of it all. No need for applause or to ask any questions about how or what is going on. Just relax and experience in awe the greatest show to have ever existed play out right in front of you.

The gift of losing your senses

I remember watching a documentary on Netflix called *Rising Phoenix*. It was about the formation and history of the Paralympics. The story of how the games came about is quite amazing, but one thing that stood out for me was the individual stories of the athletes and how most of them didn't even consider that they had a disability. They viewed their differences as strengths and they were able to see and do things that ordinary people couldn't.

This becomes more obvious when you meet someone who has had one or more of their senses taken away from them. We often pity this person yet don't consider how this apparent loss actually enriches and enhances their remaining senses. They experience a depth and sensitivity of life through their remaining active senses that those of us with all five senses rarely will. Let this be a stark reminder of how much we take our senses for granted and how shallow our experience of life often is.

We can, however, fine-tune each sense through the temporary deprivation of our other senses. You may have heard of sensory deprivation exercises. These can be a great experiences that will show you how the loss of one

We can fine-tune each sense through the temporary deprivation of our other senses.

or more of your senses heightens your remaining senses. This is also one of the reasons why we close our eyes when we meditate, so our other senses become more acute. Play around with blocking out different senses during your meditations and see how this deepens the vividness of your other senses. For example, meditate in a pitch-black room and notice how much your hearing sense comes alive or try meditating wearing noise-cancelling headphones and see how much more vivid your sight becomes. Doing this regularly trains your senses to experience and take in more of each moment. This will then add a deeper richness to your day-to-day activities and interactions.

How can meditation possibly be boring?

As you begin to explore your inner world and go on these sensory adventures, a wonderful realisation begins to form. How truly incredible and fascinating each and every moment is. How every single moment comes anew and is offering something fresh for you to observe and study. How everything at every moment is changing. Evolving. Moving. Flowing. Swirling. This constant pulse of life beating around and, literally, within you right in this moment as you are reading these words.

It's now hard for me not to laugh when I hear people say that they think meditation is boring. If only they knew about this inner-wonderland that is waiting for them to explore within each and every moment. I understand it can be easy to assume this perspective when all they see and have heard about meditation is a person sitting in a room quietly with their eyes closed. But hopefully by now you have come to agree with me that this is hardly the case.

'I shut my eyes in order to see' – I love this simple yet profound quote by the late French artist Paul Gauguin. There is so much we can 'see' by going within. Not only does everything about ourselves become clear but we also

There is so much we can 'see' by going within.

begin to see and appreciate everything around us so much more. All the things we often take for granted become fascinating, ever-changing, wondrous constructs of life.

Meditation can never be boring when you are exploring the present moment, whether that's your inner world or the world around you. How can it possibly be boring when in every moment there is something new to observe and connect with? The only way meditation can become boring is when you have unknowingly slipped out of your awareness and back into either the thinking or auto-pilot mode of the mind. If ever you find yourself saying, 'This is boring,' during meditation, it is only because you have caught yourself in either one of these modes.

When this happens, challenge yourself to find something new and interesting to connect with in the present moment. This could even be something that you've used within your meditation practice hundreds of times before. Take your breath, for example. As we've touched on a few times, our breath is one of the most popular and common elements to connect with during meditation, as it is something that is ever-present within us. But have you fully experienced all facets of your breathing within your meditation? What about noticing the different speeds you can feel and move the air through your body? Maybe there are different physical sensations that the breath has within the body that you've never noticed before. Like, have you ever felt the sensation the air has on your teeth when you breathe through your mouth? What about the feeling it has on your tongue? The lining within your mouth? Have you ever noticed how your breath expands the fabric of the clothes you're wearing which causes a subtle tingling sensation of friction between your clothes and your skin? Have you explored how deep you can take your breath into your diaphragm? Even all these factors themselves constantly change. The temperature of the air you're breathing is always changing. Whether it's because of the time of the day or night, or what's happening with the weather, or if you're inside or outside. These conditions all change the temperature of the air you're breathing in at any given moment. Therefore, every time you notice the temperature of your breath within your meditation, it will be different from the last time you noticed. A new, fresh and interesting observation for you to delight in.

We're only scratching the surface here on what we can notice about just this single process that is happening within us. Our breath is only one of the million different experiences happening in each and every moment. How can meditation possibly become boring knowing this? It can't. So go and see what you can notice and discover. The world truly is your oyster, and meditation is your ticket to explore it all.

To see a world in a grain of sand

I am yet to experience the honour of being a father. However, I have served a decent amount of time as an uncle and one of my favourite activities as an uncle is to just witness my nephews and niece in a natural habitat. I am in awe of how they can make something which is seemingly so ordinary into something so extraordinary.

Just the other day I was at the beach with them and as soon as we hit the sand, they were off exploring, finding all different types of shells, rocks and seaweed. Every few minutes they'd return with their hands full of their latest haul and dump it at my feet. Each of them would then pick up one of their newfound treasures, excitedly saying, 'Uncle Luke! Uncle Luke! Take a look at this one!'

It was just another rock.

A rock. One of the most common and ordinary things on our planet. But they were completely in awe of it.

Now, when was the last time you got excited over a rock? Every day we walk over hundreds or even thousands of them without ever noticing their significance. Yet every single rock on this planet we call home has its own story, and to contemplate this creates a powerful and humbling perspective. William Blake captured this point perfectly in his poem, 'To See a World …':

To see a World in a Grain of Sand
And a Heaven in a Wild Flower,
Hold Infinity in the palm of your hand
And Eternity in an hour.

Try this the next time you're at the beach. Grab a handful of sand and brush away as much of it as you can so you're left with just a single grain of sand in the palm of your hand. Then take a minute or so to just really observe it. Bring it up as close as possible to your eyesight and see what you can notice about this one grain of sand. Its colour. Its shape. Now think about a possible life story that this single grain of sand has gone through to get to this very moment and place of being in the palm of your hand. The story can go however you like. All I would encourage you to do is to try to go back as far as possible into the history of where this grain of sand could have come from. The story could go something along the lines of …

Fifty thousand years ago, this single grain of sand was once a part of a giant mountain in the Andes of Patagonia. A mountain that was over four thousand metres high and would take weeks to circumnavigate. It was so grand that its snow-capped summit would rarely be seen as it was constantly hidden by the clouds above. As the ice would melt each year with the changing of seasons, creeks and waterfalls would appear within the gorges, ever so slowly wearing down the mountain's rock faces into sediment that would tumble and turn all the way down the mountain into the rivers that spread across the foothills of the mighty mountain. Every hundred years or so, there would be a huge storm that would flood these plains and push all the debris out into the South Atlantic Sea. Over the next few thousand years this rock, which was once part of the giant mountain in Patagonia, rode the currents of the ocean. Bouncing and bounding along the sea floor. Becoming smaller and smaller over time due to the corrosive nature of the sea. Until one day, it washed up onto the beach you are sitting on at this very moment. Joining the millions of other grains of sand on this particular beach in this exact time. Each of which have their own story as well. But in this moment, it is just this single grain of sand that is in the palm of your hand right now. This is what William Blake meant when he wrote, 'To see a world in a grain of sand'.

There is a similar story, too, for every ordinary thing that is surrounding you right now. The wood and plastic that your furniture is made out of – what story have these gone through to get to being in their current form in your room at this time? The cotton in the clothes you're wearing. The silver or gold around your fingers. The paper in this page you are reading these words on. They all came from this earth and they all have a seemingly impossible story behind them. This newfound curiosity and deep interest in the things around you are natural by-products of practising meditation for a while. Why does this happen, though?

Because when we're meditating, we are also training ourselves in the art of observation. Whether that's observing our breath, different sensations throughout the body, or our emotions and feelings. After we've spent a decent amount of time observing our inner world, there's a natural spill-over of this into our outer world. A wonderful new way of seeing everything around us begins to emerge. A type of understanding that each and every thing happening in any given moment is truly a miracle.

Newfound curiosity and deep interest in the things around you is a natural by-product of practising meditation.

Get curious

As this new view of the world slowly begins to unfold, there are additional mindful exercises we can proactively practise that will add to this awakening. Intentionally increasing your overall level of curiosity is one such thing I would highly encourage. This can be done in a casual manner where you just bring a greater level of curiosity to any thing or situation in your day. It could be as simple as really trying to taste all the different flavours in your lunch, to really tuning in to one of your favourite songs and trying to find a sound or element of it you've never noticed before.

A more intentional exercise I like to do is what I call a 'curious walk'. Most mornings I like to go for a walk with my dog down to the local cafe to grab a coffee. I take the same route there and back most days. However, every time I do this walk now, I try to find three things I've never noticed before. It doesn't matter how many times I've done the walk before, it also doesn't matter how mundane the new thing is, as long as it is something I've never noticed before. This could be a tree, building or sign. Maybe a flower was there last week and is gone now. It really doesn't matter what they are, as long as I strive to notice three new things every time I go on my morning walk.

Also, it doesn't have to be a 'curious walk'. It could be a 'curious commute' to work. For example, if you're sitting on a bus travelling to and from work, try to find three new things you've never noticed before. Like how certain trees have managed to survive and thrive when surrounded by cement or maybe there's a few new shops that you've never noticed before. You could also start having 'curious lunch breaks'. Any time of your day that is fairly repetitive, add this 'three new things I've never noticed before' exercise to it and begin to notice the additional richness you experience each day.

Another thing I like to do now and then when I step outside my front door is to pretend my neighbourhood is a foreign land I've never visited before. Think of the times when you've travelled to a new place and how you're constantly looking around at everything, taking in as much as you can. All the things the locals seem to just rush by and ignore, while you're taking a deep interest in everything you see. The statues, the parks and surrounding nature, the tiny hidden cafes. Everything is an adventure. Try and bring this same level of curiosity to your own neighbourhood. You'll be amazed at what you notice and discover.

Adding this deeper sense of curiosity to your daily life will bring about a deeper richness and an appreciation for all the small, amazing things that we so often take for granted.

Hang out with *un*like-minded people

A term I hear a lot of in different wellness circles is 'find your tribe' or 'spend time with like-minded individuals'. Although this advice often comes from a place of good intention and, yes, initially spending time with like-minded people will help you feel safe and supported, there will come a point where spending too much time with people just like yourself will begin to work against you. It will stunt your inner growth and secretly slip you back into unawareitis. Well-intentioned sub-cultures can turn into gossip circles of comparison and competition, and unfortunately I see this a fair bit in the wellbeing space. Why do you think Jesus spent most of his time hanging out with the tax collectors and prostitutes and not with other spiritual people like the Pharisees and high priests? This is how I think a lot of religion has come undone, when the power constructs within these groups begin to overshadow the principles that first brought them together.

One thing that I found when I began practising more Stage Three types of meditations is that I started to seek out different types of people, practices and principles. This curiosity wasn't a desperate search for more, it was a type

As your general level of curiosity increases, so will your interest in trying to understand other people's perspectives and opinions.

of healthy fascination of simply wanting to experience and learn more. It's a big reason why I decided to write this book. To try to reach the non-meditation type of folk. You may begin to notice this yourself, too, after you've been practising these types of meditations for a while. As your general level of curiosity increases, so too will your interest in trying to understand other people's perspectives and opinions. This is something I fully encourage. Spend more time with unlike-minded people. You will learn so much more about yourself.

Becoming friends with death

We're going to slam the brakes on opening yourself up to noticing and appreciating all the small things in life, and talk about death for a bit. 'Way to kill the vibe, Luke.' I know, but hear me out. Death doesn't have to be something we're afraid of. It does not have to be treated as an enemy, something that we have to try and defeat to enjoy life. It is just as much a natural part of life as living is. There would be no life if there was no death. Whether that is physical life, like decaying vegetation providing the needed nutrients for new plants, trees and flowers to grow. Or figuratively, when someone gains a new lease on life after the death of a loved one. Death provides the fuel for all forms of life. It is essential for the world to function properly and stay alive.

If this is the case, why do we fear death so much? We fear it because it exposes the level of unawareness in which we've been living our own lives and how much power our attachments have over us. Both of which are very confronting realisations and therefore trigger our safety response of fear. But just like how we dealt with other difficult emotions we often experience, like anxiety and anger, fear can also be observed and dealt with in a manner that actually helps us evolve.

This powerful meditation is one not to be taken lightly. The further you allow yourself to let go and surrender to this experience, the stronger the realisations and actions will follow.

DEATH MEDITATION

Here's a guided meditation on death that I do on the first day of each month. I have found that doing some form of this type of meditation once a month maintains a level of deep appreciation for life itself and also gives me that little kick to make sure I am squeezing as much as possible out of each moment we have. I would recommend giving yourself between 20 and 30 minutes for this meditation and, if possible, a dark, private room where you can lie on your back on the floor or a bed.

Start off with closing your eyes and taking three big, deep and long breaths. Try to slow down these breaths as much as possible (ideally about ten seconds for each exhale and inhale). Allow your awareness to scan your body, starting from the crown of your head and moving all the way down to the tips of your toes. Feel the weight of your body. Notice how gravity is gently pulling you into the ground, without any force though. It is not holding you there but it is also warmly welcoming you. Are there any prominent sensations that your awareness is drawn to? If so, observe them for a few moments and actively release any tension if it's there.

See if you can notice that within your physical body there is another weightless component to you. The part of you that is your awareness. It is everywhere your physical body is but there is no solidity to this part of you. It is like a thin layer of light under your skin, ever flowing and shimmering throughout your body. Allow yourself to enter into this formless part of yourself. Notice the connection yet also the separation between your physical body and the formless energy within and around your body. How each part of you melts and works together. Complementing each other. Notice how the breath is the wonderful meeting place between this physical part of you and the formless part of you.

Use your breath now as a carrier of energy. With each inhale you are taking weight from the physical self and transmuting it into the light of your non-physical self. Continue to use your breath as this transporting vehicle between your selves until there is no more weight to carry from your physical self into your formless self. Once the weight is given to the formless self, it is processed into light. Allow your physical form to dissolve and disintegrate into the earth underneath you. Until all that is left is your formless, light body. Feel and acknowledge this separation. Don't hold on to your physical self. Let it go. Let it dissolve gracefully. Let yourself die. Let go of everything that was associated with your physical self. Your name. Your body. Your loved ones. Let it all go and allow yourself to completely float into the formless self, into the light and the vast space and atmosphere surrounding all things. Notice that you have arrived in this new space. There is a warmness to it. A beautiful welcome and deep union with all things.

Allow yourself to explore this place. Notice wherever you go you feel safe and loved. All that was weighing down your physical self has gone. You feel at peace with all and a deep love for those who meant so much to you when in your physical self. Allow yourself to observe this. In this space contemplate one or a few of the following questions and statements:

- Death is inevitable. No one is exempt.
- What do I need to do to feel at complete peace in this place?

- Death will eventually happen. Whether we are prepared for it or not.
- What in life matters?
- The human body is fragile. Each breath brings us closer to death.
- Am I at peace with this?

Contemplate these questions in this formless state. Allow yourself to really explore the answers that arise. Take as long as you need here.

Then, whenever you feel ready, begin to let your formless self bring life back into your physical self. A new, lighter version of your physical self, one that has sprouted up from the earth. Allow the new version of your physical self to merge with your formless self. One moves into the other. This union is accompanied by taking a few deep, conscious breaths. Slowly begin to open your eyes and take a few minutes to decompress the experience you've just gone through. It may help to write down anything you feel needs to be taken note of.

The rise of the sixth sense

Now that you have experienced death yourself, you'll be able to do something really cool and see other dead people. Just joking, sorry. I had you going there though, right? However, what does tend to happen after we have contemplated death long enough and opened ourselves up through our five senses to connect with and process life more, whether it be during your meditation or everyday mindful exercises, is that you may stumble upon a strange new realisation. That all along there has been another sense present. A sixth sense that has been needed in order for you to even notice one of your other five senses. This is your awareness sense. It's the formless part of you that detached from your physical body. It's the sense that does the sensing. The witness behind it all. Your soul.

This sense becomes almighty when the other five senses come together in union with one another. It's like when a bunch of superheroes combine their powers to form the ultimate warrior. This is what happens when you begin to open up your senses and allow them to merge and experience the present moment. Your sixth sense becomes whole again. A type of 'returning to home' feeling happens

This rise of your sixth sense is not something that can be bought, inherited or obtained from any external source.

and now that it is free, it wants to show you around its hometown. To take you on a journey of how to really experience life to the fullest.

This rise of your sixth sense is not something that can be bought, inherited or obtained from any external source. It can only arise from within you, through a process of developing inner calmness first (Stage One), then a liberation of our inner restraints (Stage Two) and finally through an expansion and union of our senses (Stage Three). Once we have gone through these stages, it is like we are pulled up and out of our shell to be able to see the bigger picture. We can observe not just our own situation but also the whole workings of the world around us too. Astronauts talk about a similar perspective shift to this when they are up in space looking back down on planet Earth, known as 'The Overview Effect'. When they see the whole planet as just a tiny blue and green dot floating amongst the complete darkness of space, a realisation washes over them of how all of life is connected. How this entire planet is just a shared home, without boundaries between nations, people and species. This is what happens when our sixth sense arises.

Exploring other worlds

Yes, we can even now begin to explore and visit other worlds within our meditation practice. It is one of the more unique and exciting gifts we have as humans. Welcome to the world of your imagination. A place where you can create anything you wish in your mind's eye. A place to let your creativity run wild. Whether that's painting what your ideal future looks like or creating a piece of art. Your imagination is another world you can step into any time you want to bring the invisible alive.

It is also a cool addition to your meditation practice – with emphasis on the word *addition.* I have intentionally *not* introduced imagination to the party sooner as it can often be mistaken as meditation. This is something to be mindful of as there are a lot of guided imagination experiences out there that are labelled as meditation. You may have already listened to one of these thinking it was a meditation. They usually involve taking you on some type of imaginary journey, like walking through a serene field of knee-high grass on a beautiful spring morning. This may have evoked a nice visual experience for you, but it isn't quite meditation. You are still engaged in the thinking mode of the mind here. You're imagining what could be, not connecting with what is. This is a big and important difference. Still, it is a very powerful and useful gear of the mind and, as mentioned, a great addition to enhance your experience within your meditation practice even further.

How can it do this? It does this by expanding your sensory connections.

You can invite any type of imagination experiences into your meditations. You are now at the stage with your practice to really have fun with this. Go and explore different imaginary narratives and the feelings they arouse within you. Turn what you receive and give from what you visualise into something that you can feel and connect with in the present moment. Doing these types of meditations and experiences regularly will have a flow-on effect on your everyday life too. You will tend to carry a more loving nature wherever you go because you have opened yourself up to experience these feelings during your meditations, adding a deeper richness and beauty to your day-to-day life.

WELCOMING IMAGINATION INTO MEDITATION WITH 'LOVING KINDNESS'

To try this out, start your meditation as per usual with ten or so minutes of moving the mind into the neutral gear. You can use your primary connection sense for this. Once you feel settled and established with the present moment, move to expanding your senses one at a time. Zoom in to each one of them with curious intention. Give yourself around five to ten minutes to explore this. Once you feel like you're in a safe and open state, you can now invite your imagination to join the party.

One of my favourite narratives to create with my imagination at this point is some type of 'loving and kindness' scenario. I start off with painting a detailed visual portrait of someone who means or has meant a lot to me in my life. This could be a family member, friend, mentor or teacher (alive or no longer with us) who has shown you genuine love and kindness throughout your life. Take your time to fill in the finer details you remember most about this person. This could be their smile, their eyes, maybe a particular piece of clothing they always wore. Once you have this person focused in your mind's eye, invite your other senses to fill in any missing components that may make this person seem more alive and real. Do they have a particular associated smell? Can you almost hear their voice? Begin to then paint in the surrounding environment of your choosing. This could be a familiar place you spent time with them or it could just be a beautiful landscape that comes to mind. You're the architect here. It's completely up to you.

Keep filling in these details until you have this person clearly defined in this environment, sitting or standing about a metre in front of you. They're looking into your eyes and are simply sharing their love and kindness with you. Expressing how much they wish true happiness and fulfilment for you. Providing you with any emotional support and love you feel you need in this moment. Then, with your next few breaths, feel as if you are breathing in all this good intention coming your way. Notice how this influences your body. The different sensations you feel. The emotions you experience. This process is now moving our imagination back into meditation. We have taken something created in our imagination and turned it into a feeling to connect with in the present moment. Continue to freely enjoy receiving the gifts of your imagination for as long as you like. Tears of love and joy will often join you during these beautiful moments too. Soak it all up.

A wonderful way to finish this meditation/imagination experience is to give all that love and kindness you have received back to the person who has just given it to you. With your next few breaths out, freely give all of those wonderful intentions back with each exhale. Showering this person with love and kindness, and thanking them in the process as well. Continue to share this until you feel ready to come back into our world as we know it.

The mind wanting control back

'This is silly.' 'It seems rather basic and childish.' 'What is he talking about?' These statements, or something along the same lines, could have already crossed your mind when I was taking you through any of the previous meditations. If they didn't, they still might pop up at some point in the future. It's okay if they do. It's okay if they have. They've certainly crossed my mind multiple times when going through all of this, too. 'Seeing the world in a grain of sand' at first does sound a little loopy.

They can also pop up when you're meditating. They could come in the form of something like, 'I'm over this' or 'I'm bored'. These thoughts usually arrive as an attempt of the mind to take control back. To retreat into its comfort zone. It does this as a safety mechanism to either avoid having to confront difficult emotions that will inevitably arise once the mind is in the neutral gear or because the ego has a stubborn hold on what society has conditioned you to believe. An 'I can't do that' type of position. Either way, if these thoughts do pop up, just know that they're completely natural. It's all part of the journey.

Just like the 'catch yourself' game we played when you're in the heat of the moment and feeling overwhelmed, try to see if you can catch these thoughts when/if they arise too. Then once you've caught them, thank them for trying to look out for you. After all, they don't know any better. Try to just have some fun with this exercise. It is these moments when the mind is testing us out in meditation. When things start to feel a little uncomfortable, instead of letting our minds come back in to take control of our state of being, we decide to surrender to the moment. We let go of our mind's demands, return to the connection with the here and now and dive deeper within. It is here where the breakthroughs happen. Where the source of life can do its work, where you will shed the conditioned, stubborn layers that have been holding you back from being your true, best self.

When things start to feel
a little uncomfortable,
instead of letting our
minds come back in to
take control of our state
of being, we decide
to surrender to the
moment.

Here comes the dip

I remember after that Friday morning when I had the surreal moment of connection, I was so excited to share my experience with my friends and family. When my partner woke up, there I was waiting eagerly in the kitchen with her cup of coffee ready in hand. 'Well … Let me tell you what happened this morning,' I said before spending the next 30 minutes or so excitedly trying to do just that, explaining to her the feelings and sensations I had experienced. She seemed happy for me but it soon became clear that there was no way I could fully convey the essence of what I had experienced through words and expressions. It was certainly one of those 'had to be there' kind of moments. For the rest of the day I was on such a high. Reminiscing over and over again about what happened that morning, ecstatic that I had finally 'cracked the code'.

The very next morning, I jumped out of bed so eager to meditate and experience this surreal moment again.

I had everything set up exactly the same way. It was the same time, same place, same everything. But I'm sure you can guess what happened next. Yep, it was nothing like the morning before. There I was sitting all proud-like as if it was my birthday, waiting for all my presents to arrive. None of them did, and I was left there sulking in my own confusion.

For the next half-hour or so I went through everything leading up to and during that euphoric session on that average Friday morning. Analysing it all. Checking that I'd set everything up the same. Trying to find where I went wrong. The more time I spent looking for the answer, the more I could feel myself getting frustrated. Ultimately I decided to let it go for the time being.

The following morning, still feeling hopeful but certainly not as excited, I began my meditation as per usual. After a while, though, I could feel myself getting a little agitated. I pushed through it for a couple of minutes, then wrapped up the meditation early. Feeling even more confused and disheartened this time, I started to question myself. Maybe that experience was just a one-off? But if so, what's the point of practising meditation all these years if I'm just going to experience that high only once?

I pushed on with my meditation most mornings after this but couldn't seem to recreate that magical moment I had experienced that Friday morning. This continued for a few weeks, until it got to the point where I actually wasn't enjoying meditation that much anymore. I decided I'd try one more time and then I was going to give it a break for a while. I headed into this 'last chance' meditation with a very carefree attitude. I wasn't expecting much. I was really just doing it for a bit of closure.

It was a very basic meditation as I really didn't feel like trying, to be honest. To my surprise, it ended up being an enjoyable session. It wasn't anything spectacular. Nothing like that Friday morning experience, but it was still nice. Coming out of this session it became clear to me what was going on. Why, after all these years meditating and then experiencing this surreal moment, I was struggling with my practice. I had forgotten one of the golden rules of meditation – that meditation is a process of surrendering, not attaining. Regardless of how noble the intention is, it will still never be needed for the present moment. The present moment requires nothing. It just is what it is. You can either choose to join it or not, and that's it.

This dip may be an inevitable part of every person's journey with meditation.

Looking back at this part of my journey with meditation, I now call it 'the dip'. This dip may be an inevitable part of every person's journey with meditation. Just like nature and life itself, the present moment requires an ebb and flow, ups and downs, round and round. Like tides of the ocean coming in and out, the rising and falling of the sun in accordance with the ever-revolving earth. There's this constant sharing and harmony with everything. A beautiful dance of back and forth, and there we are in the middle of it all. A passenger witnessing and experiencing this extraordinary ride of life and in order to fully grasp the lesson of surrendering to the present moment, we have to let go of all our attachments and expectations of it. As true union and harmony with life can only exist when there is complete acceptance of it.

To put this lesson into practice, one thing I do now before every time I meditate is to 'wipe the slate clean'. Meaning that I try to treat every meditation like it's the first time I've ever meditated. Even though I've been meditating for more than a decade now, I do this every time before I start. This simply involves me taking a moment before I start any one of my meditations to say to myself, 'Let's wipe the slate clean, Luke. Treat this time meditating like it's the first time you've ever meditated. Let go of any previous experiences you've felt in meditation. Let go of any expectations you are wanting this meditation to deliver. You are simply here, ready and open to connect with life. Trust in the moment.'

This wipes away any previous experiences I've had during meditation, regardless of how good or bad they were. It creates this wonderful sense of naivety where I'm not expecting anything. I'm just open to experiencing what is. This approach, combined with the subconscious mind that has been exposed to hours upon hours of meditation already, creates the perfect environment to experience the present moment to its fullest. Here is where the energy of life exists and it knows what you need. It is just a matter of letting go, opening up and trusting the moment.

The flow-on effect of letting go

The more you practise this approach of letting go of what you are wanting meditation to do for you, the more freedom you will begin to experience in all areas of your life. This is because, as we've touched on, meditation is a simulator for living your life. A training ground for what happens in your day-to-day.

Take a moment to think about some of the attachments you have in your life. These can be difficult to admit to at first but see if you can list all the things that come to mind that you're attached to. Another way of going about this is to think about all the things you're afraid or anxious of losing or failing to achieve in your life. They are all things we have attachments to. Take your partner or a loved one, for example. The thought of losing them is quite upsetting, right? When we dwell on this thought, it can evoke uncomfortable emotions within us. Jealousy being one of them; a destructive emotion that corrupts the soul. When we feel jealous, we become afraid and scheme up ways to maintain power and control the situation and, at worst, the other person. But who really has the power in this dynamic? The one who is not attached. Freedom within the mind is the greatest type of freedom we as humans can experience. Think of another thing you're afraid of losing. Maybe it's money, your work, your friends or family. These are things you have formed an attachment to and therefore, whether you're willing to admit it or not, they all have some level of control and power over you.

In order for us to fully experience genuine happiness in our lives, we need to learn how to let go of our attachments. This does not mean we have to abandon everything and everyone around us and have no boundaries. No, not at all. Just the attachment we might have with them. To be able to look at our loved ones and say without any reservation, 'You are completely free.' This is true love. Where everything becomes free to expand, evolve and deepen, including yourself.

This is why the practice of letting go within your meditation is so important and powerful. It is training you to develop a similar approach and outlook to life in the *real* world. You'll find that the things that once made you

You'll find that the things that once made you jealous will begin to disappear, enabling you to explore and develop deeper and more loving relationships.

jealous will begin to disappear, enabling you to explore and develop deeper and more loving relationships. The fear of losing what you have attained in your life disintegrates, freeing you up to direct your energy into new goals and aspirations without them having any control over you. The anxiety you would experience trying to achieve a certain level of wealth, power and recognition starts to fade away, leaving a more confident and calm presence that naturally attracts all of that which you once so desperately desired. Let go, my friend. Let go of it all and allow your true, unique and wonderful self to rise up and receive all that awaits.

AWARENESS EXPANSION

My biggest hope is that with each page turned within this book, your own level of awareness has expanded just a little. Even if you haven't had the chance yet to do all of the exercises/meditations, if you've had a moment when you've said to yourself, 'Ah, that's interesting', then I'm so grateful that this book has reached you. That means you've experienced a small moment of expanded awareness. A moment where you've been able to 'step up and out' of your thinking self and experience things as they are without any judgement. These moments of realisation are the foundation to living a truly amazing and fulfilling life.

The more awareness we bring into our day-to-day lives, the more we will begin to notice and appreciate life itself. All of the good and bad. Just as it is. Without it consuming and controlling us. Use meditation as your vehicle to achieving this. No longer will life run you. No longer will you either be blindly sprinting from one outcome to the next in desperate pursuit of fulfilment, or allowing yourself to slip into that dull, conformed complacency. No longer will you be unwell and unaware.

By developing our awareness, we begin to move ourselves into a position of genuine power and enlightenment. We have finally grabbed the torch of life to shine a light on ourselves. We are ready and free to now choose intentionally and purposefully our next step that is in line with our true self. Our real self. Our enlightened self. This new, enlightened way of living may at first seem almost unattainable, but I assure you, if you have followed the steps and stages within this book, it is not only attainable, it will inevitably be an extraordinary lifetime adventure.

'I chose the path less unaware and that made all the difference'

This new and enlightened path doesn't have to be a completely new and drastically different version from the life you are living right now. Sometimes, this light does expose major changes that need to be made. But a lot of the time, it will just bring about a deeper, richer and more appreciative experience to the life you are already living. This itself will not only completely transform your life, but all the people around you too.

You don't have to be different to be special. You don't have to suddenly choose this life path that is 'less travelled' or against everyone else's for it to be meaningful. What's most important is that it's your path. A path that is most aligned with who you are. If this is in line with the direction of where other people are going, so be it. The big difference is that you're aware of it now. You are not controlled by it or just blindly following others. You are consciously and intentionally choosing that path. That is what is most important. The great news is, because you are now aware of this path, you can also choose to step off it at any time you like and head in a different direction if you want. It's up to you. If you have taken yourself through everything we have covered in this book and come out the other side realising that the direction in which you are already heading in your life is most aligned with who you truly are, amazing! Keep going. Just make sure you keep checking in with yourself. Meditate. Continue to work on yourself and expand your overall level of awareness. This is what will make all the difference.

An interesting realisation tends to manifest when we consciously choose this path of awareness. A lot of the time we realise that we don't have to completely transform our lives. We don't have to make a drastic change to save ourselves. Sure, sometimes a trip to India is needed. But a lot of the time, it isn't. What we needed was an awakening of our awareness. A deeper appreciation for what we already have. A light shone on where we're at and who we really are.

This results in a greater depth and richness within your life. It gives you an opportunity to begin immersing yourself in and experiencing life without it passing you by. It opens you up and allows others in. The ordinary begins to become extraordinary. Choose the path of awareness and your life will never be the same.

All you have is now. Until you don't.

| | | | | | | | | | | | | | | | | | | | | | | | | | | | | | | | | | | | | | | | | |

| | | | | | | | | | | | | | | | | | | | | | | | | | | | | | | | | | | | | | | | | |

Above is a visual representation of the total average number of years someone lives for on this planet – 84. (This is only if you're fortunate enough to live in Australia. The world average is actually 72.)

This is what the total number of years left looks like if you're currently aged 35.

| | | | | | | | | | | | | | | | | | | | | | | | | | | | | | | | | | | | | | | | | |

Doesn't look like much, does it? Your whole life, shown and summarised on a single line or two.

Now you're probably thinking, 'I wasn't expecting the book to wrap up like this, Luke.' I know, and I don't mean to put a downer on things, especially as we're coming to the end of our time together. But this is my final opportunity to try to reach out and remind you how precious life is. How finite it is. How little time we really have here. Please, I am begging you to not take this life for granted. I know this may be coming across as a bit desperate and, to be honest, it is. It has to be. Life is too precious for it not to be. I have tried my utmost to give you everything I know for you to be able to break through the years upon years of conditioning that we've all been exposed to and sedated by. The torch is now in your hands, my friend. Do with it as you wish and may your life be extraordinary.

Here and now

I have seen and experienced myself that it is possible to truly live a life of genuine happiness and fulfilment. If you've followed the steps within this book – not just read, but meditated on, acted and experienced what has been recommended – your life will transform.

It's not going to be easy. We have to first accept and admit how unwell we really are. How addicted we are to the false dream of success and happiness that we've been fed. How infected we are with our own insatiability. Or conversely, how complacent and incognisant we've become. How we've settled for far less than what we truly are and deserve. These are not easy truths to acknowledge, let alone to then do something about them.

But your true self is here. It's within you at this very moment. Waiting patiently, yet so eagerly, for you to set it free and you now have everything you need to do just that. You now have the often misunderstood and highly underrated superpower of meditation, armed and ready, to use at your disposal. To help you navigate and deal with anything and everything that life throws at you. Use it at first to give yourself some space and time for relief.

Your true self is here.
It's within you at this
very moment.

The world is in desperate need of relief. Spend as much time as you need here in Stage One. Your problems and the pressures of society certainly aren't going anywhere. They'll be waiting just as eagerly for you to deal with them when you're ready.

Even when you are ready to courageously start swinging into Stage Two and dealing with all of the tricky, emotional stuff, remember, you always have access to the neutral gear whenever you need some relief.

Rest, my friend. Start with giving yourself the gift of calmness first. Learn and experience how to first move your mind away from all of its thinking and worry, and into the neutral gear where it can rest and recharge for as long as required.

Once we've learnt the skill of connecting ourselves with the safety and peace of the present moment, we can then begin to witness the circus we are caught up in. Use meditation as your vehicle to carefully move through into Stage Two of your journey. Start by noticing all the weight we have put on ourselves, what is holding us down from being our true selves. We will also finally begin to see the societal conveyor belt of conformity we have been on, it all starts to become clear. The enemy has finally been exposed and you are now in a position, armed with your renewed energy and clarity acquired from Stage One, to do something about it.

Remember to tread carefully here. Take your time and start with releasing what has been holding you down. Through observation you release it, so it has no power over you. You are beyond, behind and above it. Your true self is in control here and you can choose what you want to do next. Are there lessons to be learnt? Do you want to change the form and function of whatever has its grip on you? Can you completely let go without any resentment or guilt? Observe and ask. Observe and ask again. Keep observing until you know you're ready to act. Action from this stage can only come from a place that is aligned with your soul's intention. Keep chipping away from this place of detached awareness until you are left with a clear, open field of consciousness.

Whenever your observations become jaded or manipulated by your ego, step back into relief. Experience the beauty of the moment again. It is always there to nurture you back to truth and reality. Let it recharge you. Then when you're ready again, step back into that space of inquisitive questioning and processing of the turbulence around and within you. Remember, the sun never rises or falls. It is always there, waiting patiently, shining brightly. It is us who are spinning around it in moments of darkness.

Life is here to be celebrated. Trust the universe. Turn to your meditation practice once again in Stage Three and allow yourself to fall into the beauty of life. It is no accident why we say we're 'falling' into love. Let go of it all and you will see everything for what it is. To see the world in a grain of sand. All the intricate wonders of the universe. The union and oneness of life. It's all here, right in this very moment, waiting for us to discover and delight in it all. We can even see how struggle is necessary for growth, how death is necessary for life. Open yourself up and expand your senses to experience every aspect of life. Drench yourself in awareness. Constantly give thanks for what is. The gift of life that has been bestowed upon us all.

Throw yourself into experiencing all of life. Squeeze every last drop it has on offer, my friend. Allow your true self, your perfect soul to shine bright. Bringing light and liberation to yourself and those around you. Feel everything, aware that it all has a purpose, the purpose of bringing you home. Home, to the here and now.

Luke McLeod has become one of Australia's most popular thought leaders in mindfulness and meditation, helping thousands of people worldwide improve the quality of their lives by breaking down ancient consciousness wisdom and exercises in a way that is relatable, encouraging and achievable for the everyday person. For over two decades he has immersed himself in the teachings and practices of different meditation philosophies and techniques, including Vedic, Kundalini, Zen, Vipassana and modern mindfulness. Luke is the founder of The Mindful Life app, Soul Alive (soulalive.com.au) and works closely with high-performing athletes and executives. He is often invited to speak and consult with global brands on how to understand and implement mindfulness into today's fast-paced working world.

You can contact and connect with Luke at lukemcleod.co and on Instagram @luke.mcleod